"Ron has stood long, and knelt longer, at the foot of Calvary, in the shadow of its three crosses, in the brightness of its central one. In *Jesus, Remember Me* he brings us a dispatch of that encounter that is at once harrowing and exhilarating. He dares to defy all theological trendiness and instead to plunge us deep and hard into this truth; nothing but the blood of Jesus can wash away my sin. This is a book for those who want to be done with lesser things."

—Mark Buchanan
Author of *Your God Is Too Safe, Things Unseen,* and *The Holy Wild*

"Rarely is a book both theological and pastoral, historical, yet contemporary. Ron Corcoran has captured the passion, the power, and the purpose of the cross in a fresh and timely manner. In a day in which the church is being challenged to affirm her message with honesty and clarity, the author causes the reader to focus on the Cross, while at the same time masterfully weaves history, theology, doctrine and personal application into a powerful tool for the Church in the 21st century. Everyone seeking an encounter with the Living God needs to read this book and come face to face with the Father's Love that reaches into the heart of humanity."

—Dr. Alistair P. Petrie
Pastor and Author: *Releasing Heaven on Earth* and *Transformed*

"Ron Corcoran is an author self-confessedly compelled to write. Wondrously, we discover ourselves to be readers who are equally compelled to read. In this re-telling of Luke's original history, Ron himself tells a good story. His writing is clear and succinct, a beautiful blend of scripture, other significant voices, and his own personal experience. More importantly, his subject is enthralling, as we see revealed again the meaning of the God who died on a distant hill and left behind an empty cave."

—Michael Pountney
Former Principal of Wycliffe College, Toronto

"The busyness of parish life in an age of aggressive and militant secularism makes it easy to forget that our life has meaning. In the distractions and stress of our lives, meaning and purpose seem to evaporate. In the quiet despair of meaning in our world Ron Corcoran has intervened with the story of how God has answered for each of us the prayer '*Jesus, Remember Me.*'"

—Dr. Harry Robinson
Chaplain, Anglican Studies Program, Regent College
Former Rector, St. John's Shaughnessy, Vancouver, B.C.

JESUS, REMEMBER ME

JESUS,
REMEMBER ME

Ron Corcoran

Jesus, Remember Me
Copyright © 2004 by Ron Corcoran
All rights reserved.

Published 2004 by
Clements Publishing
213-6021 Yonge Street
Toronto, Ontario
M2M 3W2 Canada
www.clementspublishing.com

Cover art: "Greater Love Has No Man Than This," David Goatley, CIPA SFCA. David is currently represented by Portrait Brokers of America, The Portrait Group, Portraits North and Portraits by Artists Inc. in the US, and by Fine Art Commissions Ltd in the UK.

Lyrics from "Too Small a Price" (pp. 20-23) quoted by special permission of Don Francisco and Coronation Music Ltd.

Unless otherwise noted, all Scripture quotations are from the New International Version of the Bible, copyright © 1973, 1978 by the International Bible Society. Used by permission of Zondervan Publishers.

National Library of Canada Cataloguing in Publication Data

Corcoran, Ron
    Jesus, remember me / Ron Corcoran.

    Includes bibliographical references.
    ISBN 1-894667-43-3

    1. Jesus Christ—Crucifixion—Sermons. 2. Jesus Christ—Resurrection—Sermons. 3. Sermons, Canadian (English). 4. Anglican Church of Canada—Sermons. 5. Spiritual life—Anglican Communion—Sermons. I. Title.

BX5615.C68J48 2004   232.96'3   C2004-901447-1

CONTENTS

Dedicated to
The Praying Saints and Servants of
St. Matthias Anglican Church
Victoria, British Columbia

WHO DELIVERED UP JESUS TO DIE?
NOT JUDAS, FOR MONEY;
NOT PILATE, FOR FEAR;
NOT THE JEWS, FOR ENVY;
BUT THE FATHER, FOR LOVE!

Octavius Winslow, *No Condemnation in Christ Jesus*, 1857

ACKNOWLEDGEMENTS

A book is never written in isolation. This work has been over 20 years in the making and during that time, many saints have touched my life. They have encouraged me, prayed for me and stood by me in times of trial and tribulation, and to them I owe a tremendous debt of gratitude that mere words could never express. There are some, though, that truly deserve special recognition, and to them I would say that what you are holding in your hands is a visible expression of the fruit of my life in Christ. Thank you for being part of my journey for you have influenced me to become a "man of the Cross."

Father Daniel Matheson, it was through your ministry that I genuinely experienced the love of God the Father, embraced Jesus as Lord, and began to grow in the power of the Holy Spirit. Becca and Kandy, you have been vessels of God's love and instruments of His healing and restoration—God used your skills to "bring me to my senses." You took me out of the darkness and into God's marvellous light.

Lana, God bless you for your many hours of labour in researching all that could be found on the Cross of Christ. To my dear sister Maria, thank you for your many hours of computer expertise—can you imagine how much longer it would have taken me without your assistance?

Archbishop Reginald Hollis, Dr. Don Schurman, and Rev. Dr. Harry Robinson, to you I offer my sincere appreciation because I know that without your encouragement, wisdom and prayers, this work would not have seen the light of day.

I am forever indebted to my editors, Lynne and Michael Damant. You took what I had written and made it into a much better book. Glory to God, your prayers and dedication to this work, went far beyond what I could have asked for or ever imagined. At the end of the day, however, the author bears full responsibility for any errors or omissions.

To the congregation of St. Matthias—thank you for the time of rest, reflection and writing. You are truly a people of love and acceptance who challenge me continually to grow as a disciple, pastor and teacher.

Deirdre, my darling wife, I offer bouquets of roses to you. God has used you to show me that "there is a place where dreams come true." Thank you for your love, encouragement and patience, which sustain me throughout all my endeavours.

A special word of thanks to the artist, David Goatley, for his permission to use his art, "Greater Love Has No Man Than This." This work added the finishing touches to this labour of love.

I wish to acknowledge Rob Clements of Clements Publishing in Toronto, Ontario for his encouragement and sense of adventure in reaching out to this first time author.

Finally, praise and glory to our Lord Jesus Christ. By His grace and love, He showed me that when I called, He did "Remember Me."

Ron Corcoran
2004

FOREWORD

St. Paul wrote that the cross was a "stumbling block to Jews and foolishness to Gentiles" (1 Corinthians 1:23). This is still true. In our western culture Jesus' action of throwing his life away on the cross just does not make sense. Our society encourages us to look after ourselves, to save ourselves.

Yet St. Paul declared that he preached, "Christ crucified," for to believers, Christ was "the power of God and the wisdom of God" (1 Corinthians 1:24). The centre of the church's teaching has always been "Christ crucified".

Although to many the cross looks like a disastrous defeat, the Christian good news (or gospel) would be meaningless without the cross. The cross is the ultimate sign of God's love for us. By Jesus' offering of himself to this ignominious death, our sins are forgiven and we are brought to peace with God, the course and meaning of all life. We can take that for granted, or we can let the power of the cross change our thinking and open our hearts to God's wisdom and love.

The Rev. Ron Corcoran knew that he had often taken the cross for granted. Given the opportunity of a six-month sabbatical, he knew that he must come to the cross in a deeper way. He turned again to the study of Holy Scripture. He read the writings of the saints. He prayed and focused on the power of the cross. This study changed him as he saw in a new way what Christ had done for him on the cross.

This book is the result of the powerful effect that a concentrated study of the cross has had on Ron's life. In it he shares new insights and a personal perception of theological truths. It is his hope and his prayer that others will be blessed as they also come to know the power of the cross in a new way.

There can never be enough written about the power, wisdom, love and mercy of God revealed in the cross.

Reginald Hollis
Archbishop of Montreal (Retired)

INTRODUCTION

Jesus did many other things as well. If every one of them was written down, I suppose that even the whole world would not have room for the books that would be written. (John 21:25)

John the Apostle by the grace of God was able to see down the ages and his prophetic words have proven to be absolutely correct. There is not enough room in our world for the books that have been and will be written about Jesus. Like millions who have gone before me, I write because I am compelled to write. The seeds for the writing of this book were planted in my heart over twenty years ago, but it took that long for them to come to fruition. The Catholic theologian, priest and writer Henri Nouwen, said: "Writing is a process in which we discover what lives in us. The writing itself reveals what is alive…The deepest satisfaction of writing is precisely that it opens up new spaces within us of which we were not aware before we started to write. To write is to embark on a journey whose final destination we do not know."[1] Like John, Henri Nouwen has also proven to be correct.

I have found that the journey I have been on for the past two years has been life-changing. Like others, I have discovered that no one can write about the cross, without the cross having a profound effect on their inner being. Since beginning this writing, I have discovered what is alive in the deep recesses of my soul. My passion for God, for Jesus and for the cross has come alive in a brand new way. Once again I stand in awe of the grace, mercy and love of God that were demonstrated in the life and ministry of the Lord Jesus Christ. I have been overwhelmed with God's love and passion for our hurting world.

At one time, I thought that the cross of Jesus was only about suffering, shame and guilt. The love of God supposedly displayed on the cross did not reach out to embrace me. It repelled me. What I didn't realize was that I was looking only at the surface. My prayer for you as you read this book is that you will discover that the cross of Jesus Christ is not about endless suffering, shame and guilt. It is about God's eternal plan of redemption. It is about His forgiveness, grace and mercy. But most of all, it is about God's overwhelming love for this world and for each of us—His beloved children.

When I started writing this book, I had three sets of readers in mind. Is it possible for one book to reach out and touch three different audiences? I believe it is. I write for those who have always stumbled over the cross—those who have found the cross and its message repulsive as I once did. I write also for those who are wondering in our scientific and technological age if the cross is relevant any longer. Do we still need "the old rugged Cross" to find our way home to God? I write as well for those who have encountered and embraced the message of the cross. This book will re-affirm your beliefs in a God who, for the sake of love, was willing to suffer and die for all humanity.

According to the biblical record, on the day that Jesus died, two thieves or malefactors or criminals were crucified with Him. All three were crucified outside the gates of Jerusalem at a place called

16

Golgotha, the Place of the Skull, or Calvary Hill. On the day we now call Good Friday, there were three crosses on a hill. Behind each cross lies a story. On the centre cross hung Jesus the Christ, the Son of the living God, who came into this world to die so that we could be reconciled with our Heavenly Father. This cross tells the story of God's free offer of Redemption to humanity. On the cross to Jesus' right hung a criminal, one who at the very last moment of his life reached out to accept redemption. This is the cross of Reception, and you can be assured from the Gospel account that the thief who was on this cross now walks the golden streets of Paradise. On the cross to Jesus' left hung another criminal, one who spent his last hours of life railing against Jesus. This is the cross of Rejection, and the thief who was on that cross shunned any possible future with his suffering companions.

Within the Gospel of Luke, in his account of the events of Jesus' crucifixion, is a treasure that I believe must be brought forth. It is only in Luke's Gospel that we find any detail of the two who were crucified with Jesus.

I have mentioned that the compulsion to write a book about these events uniquely described by Luke, first stirred in my heart almost twenty years ago. In the mid-eighties, I heard a song by the Christian artist, Don Francisco, called "Too Small A Price." This song tells the story of that dreadful day of the Crucifixion from the perspective of one of the criminals. Through the ages this criminal who was crucified with Jesus came to be known as "the repentant thief" or "the good thief." The dramatic account in the song of what happened to him bound me to the story in Luke's Gospel. The words of the song appear at the end of this introduction, and I am grateful to Don and Wendy Francisco for their permission to use them here. I hope they will bless you as they have blessed me. This CD is still available at <www.rockymountainministries.org>. The whole CD is well worth adding to one's musical collection.

In 1992, I was in Edinburgh, Scotland and had a moment to visit an art gallery that featured an exhibition on the life of Christ. In this gallery, I found a work that completely overwhelmed me. It was a painting of the crucifixion of Jesus and the two others who were crucified with Him. It was immediately obvious that those who hung on the crosses were dead. In the clouds behind each cross came angelic beings. Over the figure of Jesus and one of those crucified with Him, were angels in robes of white with their arms outstretched to transport them, it seemed, from the cross to paradise. Behind the other crucified figure were dark angelic beings, also with arms outstretched to transport him. I was deeply moved that this artist had put on canvas the subject of the story that had long been in my heart to write. At the time, I was too awestruck to note the artist's name or history. Over the years I have tried without success to track down a copy of the painting or even the name of the artist. I continue to search.

The primary reason for writing this story is the remembrance of the hunger and thirst within my soul to find God. I share the outcome of that story in this book. When I reflect back almost twenty-five years ago, I was a desperate man on a desperate search. I needed to know that God existed, and that He had a reason and a purpose for my existence. I truly wanted to know if God remembered me, for I was lost. The cry of "the good thief" was the cry of my heart. "Jesus, Remember Me."

Philip Yancy, one of my favourite authors, writes in his book *Soul Survivor,* that any writer, but especially a writer of faith, offers: "a unique perspective of creation, a point of view visible only from the point where I am."[2] That is the gift that I offer you.

I know it would have been impossible to write this book, however, without the assistance of other writers who, down through the centuries, shared their insights about the cross. I have benefited tremendously from their work and in this book, I have shared with you some of their wisdom and knowledge. To each of these writers, I will be eternally indebted.

I pray that God the loving Father will accept this offering of writing from my hand and use it to bless others, as I have been so richly blessed.

Ron Corcoran
Victoria, British Columbia

TOO SMALL A PRICE

I awoke to hear the jailor turn the key and push the door
"Get out here" he shouted, but I stayed there on the floor
Frozen in the terror that rose and filled my brain
For I knew what they intended
I could not face the pain.

Then soldiers came into the cell and they dragged me to the
    yard
They threw me down before a cross and brought the whip
    down hard
"Carry it," they shouted as I struggled to my feet
I put my shoulder under it and dragged it to the street.
I stumbled through a wall of screams as they drove me through
    the gate.

It seemed that thousands lined the streets
Their voices filled with hate
Like a wolf-pack in the night that moves in for a kill
They closed the gap and followed us as we started up the hill.

And it seemed I barely reached the top when they grabbed me
    from behind
They threw the cross down under me and tied the ropes that
    bind
The arms close to the beams as they nailed the feet and hands
And they raised the cross up in the air and dropped it in its
    stand.

Through a blur of pain I saw the cross there next to mine
There were people all around it so I looked to read the sign
It was nailed there up above his head so the world could see
    the news

That the man who seemed so helpless there was the King of all
    the Jews.
And the crowd that stood around his cross made jokes about
    his name
They shouted, laughed and spat on Him so I joined in the
    game
I said, "Hey if you're the King why don't you get us down
    from here?"
But the taunt just sounded hollow, it echoed in my ears
'Cause he looked at me with eyes that seemed to reach into my
    heart

They shone a light on all my lies and tore my life apart
There was more that lay behind that gaze than simple blood
    and clay
But knowing was too much for me, I had to look away.
But I chanced another look at Him while He was looking
    down
Where the soldiers who'd just crucified us drank there on the
    ground
And although He spoke them quietly somehow His words
    came through
He said, "Father, please forgive them, they don't know what
    they do."
Then as if they'd heard Him speaking the crowd began to roar
Whipped into a frenzy by the priests who urged them on
    to more
But the worse the accusations now the plainer I could see
The guilt of the accusers, not the one there next to me.
But the man upon the other cross began to curse and swear
And his voice was filled with venom as he hurled it through
    the air
All the horror that was in him and had laid his life to waste
Came out in every syllable he flung in Jesus' face
Jesus only looked at him but something rose inside of me

JESUS, REMEMBER ME

In spite of all that watched us there, it couldn't be denied
Because His righteousness and innocence were shining bright
    and strong
I just couldn't keep my silence if that cursing still went on
I cried out "Don't you fear the wrath of God even at the end
You'll curse us both into the pit, is that what you intend?
We're only getting what we're due, we sinned our whole lives
    long
But don't you talk to Him that way, 'cos he's done nothing
    wrong!"

And then with all my courage and in a voice not quite my own
I asked Him "Lord, remember me when you come into your
    throne"
He answered me and even then His love was undisguised
He said "Before the sun has set today you'll be with me in
    paradise."
The shouts and curses did not stop even when the sunlight
    ceased
But somehow in the midst of it my soul had been released
Though the agony continued it was still too small a price
To be allowed to hear those words and to die beside the
    Christ.

Then darkness changed to dawning
And I heard the sound of voices
The air was warm around me
I stood beside a stream
And Abraham was speaking
To the multitudes before him
At the unfolding of the answer
To our prayers and hopes and dreams
And far across the chasm
Came a rumbling like the thunder
And the Prince of Peace came shining

From His mouth the power streamed
And the walls and towers crumbled
And the gates of hell went under
As thousands sang the victory
We have been redeemed
Jesus is the Lord of all
Jesus is the Lord of all
Jesus is the Lord of all
We have been redeemed. [3]

CHAPTER 1

A Hidden Treasure In
The Gospel of Luke

For my eyes have seen your salvation, which you have prepared in
the sight of all people, a light for revelation to the Gentiles and for
glory to your people Israel. (Luke 2:30-32)

I am embarrassed to confess that the first Bible that came into my
possession was stolen. I know because I stole it! I was in my early
twenties and searching for some meaning to my existence. I thought
that if I could get my hands on a Bible, I would be able to solve some
of the mysteries of life. I did not think of buying one. I didn't dare
to go into a store and ask for one. I thought that if I attempted to
buy a Bible, the store clerks would tell me I was not allowed to have
one. I had grown up in a church that did not encourage its laity to
own or to even read a Bible, for fear of misinterpretation. So I did the
only thing I could, in an act of quiet desperation I slipped into one
of those other churches that had Bibles in every pew and stole one.
They had so many I didn't think they would miss one. There would
have been no need to worry about my misinterpreting it, because I

couldn't even understand it! I had stolen a copy of the King James Version of the Bible and its Old English was chock-full of *thees*, *thous* and lists of *begats*.

Since I couldn't understand what I was reading, I stuck it under my pillow and hoped that by osmosis it would seep into my brain and I would glean great knowledge about God. It didn't work! Even though I had stolen that first Bible, today I remain convinced that God honoured my first feeble attempts to gain knowledge and understanding of Him. I think He saw within me a genuine thirst and hunger for Him.

You may be shocked to read that I stole a Bible, but in the pages of this book, I want to tell you a story about another thief who, by all accounts, had spent his whole life stealing, but by the amazing grace of God ended up in paradise.

The story of the thief who turned to Jesus in the last hours of his life is unique and one of the many treasures we find in Luke's Gospel. Although all four Gospels record that there were two others crucified with Jesus, Luke is the only one who tells this story of salvation. Matthew records: "*In the same way the robbers who were crucified with him also heaped insults on him*" (Matthew 27:44). Mark says: "*Those crucified with him also heaped insults on him*" (Mark 15:32b). John the Apostle doesn't record any words from the lips of the crucified thieves, he simply says: "*Here they crucified him and with him two others—one on each side and Jesus in the middle*" (John 19:18). So why does Luke tell a different story and how do we know it is accurate?

Biblical scholars acknowledge that Luke was a careful historian. Therefore, we can be sure that the teachings, parables and stories contained in the Gospel that bears his name are accurate. In fact, at the very beginning of his Gospel, Luke tells us why he wrote this Gospel and why we should trust its accuracy:

> *Many have undertaken to draw up an account of the things that have been fulfilled among us, just as they were handed down to us by those who from the first were eyewitnesses and servants of the word.*

Therefore, since I myself have carefully investigated everything from the beginning, it seemed good also to me to write an orderly account for you, most excellent Theophilus, so that you may know the certainty of the things you have been taught. (Luke 1:1-4)

Why does Luke tell a different story than do the other Gospel writers? I caution the members of my congregation that when reading Scripture, they must always put it in context. A verse of Scripture does not stand alone, but is always supported and affirmed by other passages of Scripture. We need to put Luke's Gospel in context and that will help unravel the mystery as to why he is the only Gospel writer who tells this story of the repentant thief.

We know from history, and Paul's Letter to the Colossians, that Luke was a physician. In his account of the Acts of the Apostles, Luke tells us that he was Paul's companion on a number of his missionary journeys. One cannot help but notice that Pauline theology is evident throughout Luke's Gospel. We also know that Luke was a Gentile and therefore he is the only New Testament writer who was not Jewish. When reading the Gospels we must remember that each Gospel has a distinct character.

Matthew's Gospel was written to Jewish believers to convince them that Jesus was the long awaited Messiah. Much of Matthew's Gospel is focused on the Old Testament prophecies that foretold the coming of the Messiah and shows how these Messianic prophecies were fulfilled in Jesus. Mark's is the simplest of the four Gospels and emphasizes the humanity of Jesus. Some have described Mark's Gospel as a biography of Jesus since he tells the story of Jesus' life in a simple and dramatic fashion. Scholars say that John's Gospel is the theological Gospel written for the Church. Its overall purpose was to prove conclusively that Jesus is the Son of God. Luke's Gospel, on the other hand, is viewed as the universal Gospel. He, more than any other writer, lets us know that God's gift of salvation is available to all humanity. It is Luke who reminds us that Jesus said, *"People will come from the east and west and north and south and take their places at the feast in the kingdom of God"* (Luke 13:29).

In writing this Gospel, Luke wants us to understand that nationality, race, gender, and social position are not deterrents to receiving God's grace. But at the same time, this Gospel is also very particular. Luke makes it clear that it is only those who place their trust in Jesus who will inherit eternal life. Luke portrays Jesus as the hope not only of the nation of Israel, but also of the whole world. That is reflected in a number of ways. When Matthew traces Jesus' earthly genealogy, he goes back as far as Abraham. Luke on the other hand traces that genealogy all the way back to Adam, who is our universal ancestor. All four Gospel writers quote from Isaiah chapter 40, when they are speaking of the prophecy of John the Baptist, *"Prepare the way for the Lord, make straight paths for him"* (Isaiah 40:3-5). Luke however, is the only one to include all of that prophecy which continues with the words, *"And all mankind will see God's salvation"* (Luke 3:4-6). Luke is the only Gospel writer who includes the story of Simeon and his prophecy concerning Jesus as God's gift of salvation, not only for the nation of Israel, but also for the Gentile people. When Jesus was presented at the Temple, Simeon took Him in his arms and blessed Him and praised God, saying, *"Sovereign Lord, as you have promised, you now dismiss your servant in peace. For my eyes have seen your salvation, which you have prepared in the sight of all people, a light for revelation to the Gentiles and for glory to your people Israel."* (Luke 2:29-32) Yes, Jesus was sent to the lost nation of Israel, but Luke as the writer of this *universal* Gospel underscores that Jesus was the Redeemer of both Jews and non-Jews. In fact, Luke goes to great pains to show us that Jesus' message was not limited, but available to all who receive and accept God's message of salvation.

There are many other unique characteristics of Luke's Gospel and although I don't have room to list them all, I would like to mention a few. Luke's Gospel emphasizes Jesus' prayer life (Luke 3:21; 5: 16; 6:12; 9:18; 9:29; 23:46). Throughout his Gospel Luke gives a prominent place to women. Luke alone tells the story of Jesus' birth from Mary's point of view (1:26-38); he is the only one who records the story of Elizabeth, the mother of John the Baptist (1:5-24; 39-45); he tells the story of Anna when Jesus is presented at the temple (2:21-40); Luke is the only Gospel writer to tell the story of the woman at Nain whose only child was raised from the dead (7:11); and Luke alone, is the only writer who tells of the woman who anointed Jesus' feet at the home of Simon the Pharisee (7:36-39). It is in Luke's Gospel where you will find the three great hymns of the Church, the *Magnificat* (1:46-55), the *Benedictus* (1:68-79) and the *Nunc Dimittis* (2:29-32)—hymns that the Church continues to use daily.

Some biblical scholars and writers have described Luke's Gospel as the Gospel for the underdog. Luke is careful to show that, much to the astonishment and bewilderment of the teachers of the law, the Scribes and Pharisees, Jesus was a friend to outcasts and sinners. These religious leaders always accused Jesus of welcoming sinners and eating with them. Jesus told them very clearly, *"It is not the healthy who need a doctor, but the sick. I have not come to call the righteous, but sinners to repentance"* (Luke 5:30-32; 7:34; 15:1-2).

Luke's Gospel also contains several parables that the other Gospels omit, including those of the Good Samaritan and the Prodigal Son. The first parable reveals the sympathetic mercy and tenderness God expects us to extend to one another regardless of a person's background or social standing. The second reveals the compassionate nature and character of the heavenly Father that Jesus came to reveal to all humanity.

Another story, which is recorded in this Gospel only, is the story of Zacchaeus, the tax collector. His occupation was to collect taxes from his own people to support the Roman Empire, which oppressed the nation of Israel. There can be no doubt that Zacchaeus was one of the marginalized of Jesus' day. Jesus went to his home and without even a word from Jesus, Zacchaeus repented of his wrong actions and offered to give half his riches to the poor and to return four times what he had robbed from others. It was in Zacchaeus' house that Jesus proclaimed, *"Today, salvation has come to this house, because this man, too, is a son of Abraham. For the Son of Man came to seek and save what was lost"* (Luke 19:9-10).

Luke's Gospel highlights Jesus' genuine concern for the poor and the downtrodden, His concern for those who, because of their nationality, race, gender or social status, had become marginalized. Jesus' primary mission was the salvation of sinners, and that mission did not end when He was nailed to the cross. In the midst of His agony, pain and suffering, Jesus heard the voice of one more lost sheep. So it is not surprising that it is the historian Luke who tells us the story of the thief who turned to Jesus and asked to be remembered in the kingdom to come.

The theme of *Salvation* is the golden thread that runs from the beginning to the end of this Gospel. At the beginning of the Gospel, Mary is told, *"You will be with child and give birth to a son, and you are to give him the name of Jesus"* (Luke 1:31). The name Jesus means, "Jehovah is salvation" or "Yahweh saves." Then, after Jesus was born, an angel appeared to the shepherds and told them about the birth of the Christ-child, *"Don't be afraid. I bring you good news of great joy that will be for all the people. Today in the town of David a Saviour has been born to you; he is Christ, the Lord"* (Luke 2:10-11).

Another example of Jesus' message of salvation occurs at the very beginning of His ministry. Jesus went into his hometown synagogue and read a passage from the prophet Isaiah: *"The Spirit of the Lord is on me, because he has anointed me to preach good news to the poor. He has sent me to proclaim freedom for the prisoners and recovery of sight for the blind, to release the oppressed, to proclaim the year of the Lord's favour"* (Luke 4:18-19). Then Jesus said, *"Today this scripture is fulfilled in your hearing"* (Luke 4:21). Luke emphasizes the rejection that, from the beginning of His ministry, Jesus endured from the very people He came to save. Luke hints at the far reaching implications of Jesus' ministry when he continues Jesus' discourse to the crowd in the synagogue,

> *"I tell you the truth, no prophet is accepted in his hometown. I assure you that there were many widows in Israel in Elijah's time, when the sky was shut for three and a half years and there was a severe famine throughout the land. Yet Elijah was not sent to any of them, but to a widow in Zarephath in the region of Sidon. And there were many in Israel with leprosy in the time of Elisha the prophet, yet not one of them was cleansed—only Naaman the Syrian."* All the people in the synagogue were furious when they heard this. They got up, drove him out of the town, and took him to the brow of the hill on which the town was built, in order to throw him down the cliff. But he walked right through the crowd and went on his way. (Luke 4:24-30)

Jesus' ministry of teaching, healing and the proclamation of the Good News was directed primarily towards God's chosen people. Luke, however, by using these Old Testament examples of healing for the Gentiles in the days of the prophets reveals to us that God's eternal plan of salvation is not limited but is available to all who will receive it.

The theme of salvation is emphasized in Luke's description of the events that took place at the foot of the cross. He tells us that while Jesus was on the cross, He was taunted three times about salvation. He was challenged three times to save Himself *from* the cross. The first taunt came from the rulers and the leaders of the people: The people stood watching, and the rulers even sneered at him. They said, *"He saved others; let him save himself if he is the Christ of God, the Chosen One"* (Luke 23:35). The second taunt came from the soldiers who carried out the crucifixion: *"The soldiers also came up and mocked him. They offered him wine vinegar and said, 'If you are the king of the Jews, save yourself'"* (Luke 23:36). The third taunt came from one of those who were crucified with Jesus: *"One of the criminals who hung there hurled insults at him: 'Aren't you the Christ? Save yourself and us!'"* (Luke 23:39). All those who taunted Jesus on the cross were convinced that salvation meant liberation from the cross. Although they may not have fully realized it, all these taunts were demonic in tone. In chapter 4 of his Gospel, Luke tells us that just before Jesus began His ministry, He was tempted by the devil on three different occasions with these words, *"If you are the Son of God..."* At the end of His earthly ministry and life, He heard again these similar mocking words, *"If you are the King of the Jews..."* Thanks be to God that Jesus did not come down from the cross to save Himself, for if He had, we would all be lost. I will examine the reasons Jesus did not come down from the cross in the chapter entitled "The Cross of Redemption."

Luke is the only evangelist to include the story of the thief who turned to Jesus in the final hour of his life. I thank God that Luke included this treasure, for truly it is a story of genuine salvation. It is a story about the grace of God in action. The Gospels would be poorer without it.

CHAPTER 2

THE CROSS OF RECEPTION

One of the criminals who hung there hurled insults at him: "Aren't you the Christ? Save yourself and us!" But the other criminal rebuked him. "Don't you fear God," he said, "since you are under the same sentence? We are punished justly, for we are getting what our deeds deserve. But this man has done nothing wrong." Then he said, "Jesus, remember me when you come into your kingdom." Jesus answered him, "I tell you the truth, today you will be with me in paradise." (Luke 23:39-43)

The Scriptures are silent on the names of the two thieves who were crucified on either side of Jesus on the day we now call Good Friday, and do not identify who was on the right or the left. Tradition has it that Dismas was the repentant or "good" thief and hung on Jesus' right. It is believed he became "good" because he turned to Jesus in the last moments of his life and was saved. Tradition has it that Gestas was the thief who rejected Jesus and hung on His left. I will use those two names, as I believe they help us more easily identify the two men who were crucified next to Jesus.

Down through the centuries, Dismas' name has been kept alive and he has become known as the patron saint of prisoners. In fact there are a number of places of worship around the world named after St. Dismas. One such is the Charismatic Episcopal Cathedral of St. Dismas located in Orlando, Florida. Its Rector and lay people are recognized pioneers in the field of prison reform and they reach out to those who are in prison and work with those who have been released. At Fountain Prison in Atmore, Alabama there is a St. Dismas community. This community is made up of imprisoned men who, despite their imprisonment, are serving the worldwide Church through their prayers and outreach to others. In Kingston, Ontario, you will find a Roman Catholic Church named Church of the Good Thief. This church has been in existence since 1894. The building is constructed of native limestone quarried by the prisoners of Kingston Penitentiary and carried by them to the Church site.[1]

The Gospel writers have supplied very few details of how these two ended up being crucified next to Jesus. The synoptic Gospels tell us, however, that Dismas and Gestas were robbers or criminals. If they were robbers, they could not have been ordinary robbers. Under the Roman justice system, simple robbery was not punishable by death. The Greek word Matthew uses to describe these two is *lestes*, which means "one who uses violence to rob openly." So we can safely conclude that these two were violent criminals who were punished justly for their deeds. As we look further at these two men, we need to be clear about their characters. Although tradition, history and legend have called Dismas the "good thief," there was nothing good about either man. There were no obvious differences between them prior to their crucifixion. They were hardened, rebellious criminals who had been tried in a court of law and found guilty for their crimes against humanity. There is nothing to suggest that they were being punished unjustly. They had shared a life of crime and they were now dying together. It is in the act of dying where the differences between these two criminals come to light.

There is no suggestion in Scripture that either of these two men had encountered Jesus before this day. It is also unlikely that they had heard Jesus preach. But on this Good Friday, they saw a living sermon with Jesus using very few words to convey messages of empathy and forgiveness. The three men were linked together for they had received the sentence of death. As they made their way through the streets they were dead men walking. All three had been flogged—Jesus most severely. All three were guarded by soldiers and followed for the most part by taunting crowds. Dismas and Gestas more than likely walked behind Jesus carrying their own crosses to Calvary Hill. So their first encounter with Jesus was under circumstances of weakness and disgrace. They saw Jesus stumbling through the streets of Jerusalem beneath the weight of His cross as it pressed down upon His lacerated shoulders. On the way to Calvary they saw Jesus and listened as He set aside His own suffering to warn the daughters of Jerusalem of the evils that one day would befall their beloved city.

> *A large number of people followed him, including women who mourned and wailed for him. Jesus turned and said to them, "Daughters of Jerusalem, do not weep for me, weep for yourselves and for your children. For the time will come when you will say, 'Blessed are the barren women, the wombs that never bore and the breasts that never nursed!' Then "they will say to the mountains, "Fall on us!" and to the hills, "Cover us!"" For if men do these things when the tree is green, what will happen when it is dry?"* (Luke 23: 27-31)

These two trailing behind Jesus noticed that He took the time to comfort those who were weeping for Him. They might even have been jealous of Jesus receiving these tears, for there was no one there to weep or be concerned for them.

Luke tells a different story than does Matthew or Mark. Matthew and Mark tell us that both men hanging from their crosses heaped insults and abuse on Jesus. That may have been so at the beginning, but Luke's narrative tells us that something happened to Dismas that changed his heart and attitude toward Jesus. What could have caused that change? Could it have been these next words that Jesus spoke from the cross? Luke writes: "*Jesus said, 'Father, forgive them, for they do not know what they are doing.'*" (Luke 23:34). Normally those who were crucified spent their time cursing their tormentors. Dismas and Gestas could not have helped but wonder what kind of man was hanging from that centre cross that he would pray for those who tortured him. Jesus did not pray for Himself nor did He ask to be removed from the cross or even to be delivered from the great agony and suffering He was enduring. Instead He was praying for those who had brought this crucifixion to pass. Who would be included in the prayer of forgiveness?

Jesus would have asked His Father to forgive the religious leaders of His day, the Scribes, the Pharisees and the teachers of the law who carried the responsibility for the spiritual well being of the nation. Many of them were now gathered at the foot of the cross inciting the crowd to jeer and curse the One who hung on the cross. From the start of Jesus' ministry to the very end, they stood in opposition to Him. They hardened their hearts against Him and on many occasions they had plotted to put Jesus to death. When they finally arrested Him, they put Him through a travesty of a trial and then brought about His execution by threatening the Roman Governor with a denunciation to the Emperor. As we read the Gospel narratives it is not hard to see as Pilate did, that the clergy acted out of hatred, envy and malice: "*For he knew it was out of envy that they had handed Jesus over to him*" (Matthew 27:18). They had blood on their hands and they needed to be forgiven. Although they did not have full awareness of the significance of what they were doing, they were still responsible. On the Day of Pentecost, Peter acknowledged their ignorance in having Jesus put to death, but still held them responsible (Acts 3:17).

Jesus asked His Father to forgive the Romans. This included the soldiers who were carrying out the duty imposed upon them by the proper authority. The cruelty that Jesus endured at their hands, however, was reprehensible. We catch a glimpse of that torture in

Isaiah chapter 50: "*I offered my back to those who beat me, my cheeks to those who pulled out my beard; I did not hide my face from mocking and spitting*" (Isaiah 50:6). Although all prisoners were subjected to horrific punishment, I submit that the Gospels and the writings of the Prophets indicate that Jesus' torture went far beyond that which any normal prisoner would have had to tolerate.

Along with forgiving the Roman soldiers, Jesus forgave Pilate. According to the Gospels, on three separate occasions Pilate declared Jesus to be innocent of all charges. Yet when Pilate was faced with denunciation to the Emperor, he capitulated and sentenced Jesus to death. Although His enemies had succeeded in bringing about Jesus' crucifixion, the cross did not paralyze His pardoning power. Earlier in Luke's Gospel, Jesus said that He had the authority to forgive sins. (Luke 5:24) Even at the point of death, He used that authority to the Glory of His Father. Throughout His ministry, Jesus granted forgiveness to those who sought restoration with God. He was willing to forgive the fallen and, here on the cross, He showed that He is more than willing to grant this gift of forgiveness even to criminals and murderers, "*Father, forgive them…*" (Luke 23:34).

I believe furthermore, that Jesus' prayer was not limited to those who were directly involved. I believe that His prayer extends down through the ages to all sinners. It could be said that all sinners "do not know what they are doing" because they do not have a full realization or understanding of the malice of sin. I will say more about this in the chapter on the Cross of Redemption. What is amazing about this first word from the cross is that not only did Jesus pray for them, He made an excuse for them, "*they do not know what they are doing.*"

Both Matthew and Mark indicate that at the beginning, both criminals on the cross "heaped insults on Jesus." Try to imagine insulting the person dying next to you and hearing that person ask God to "forgive you, for you did not know what you were doing." One would think that even the most hard-hearted would be moved to compassion. Maybe it was those words that penetrated and changed the heart of Dismas.

In Luke's Gospel we read that Jesus said, *"But I tell you who hear me: Love your enemies, do good to those who hate you, bless those who curse you, pray for those who mistreat you"* (Luke 6:27-28). Jesus didn't just teach these words, he modeled them to the criminals who were hanging there with Him.

It could have been the words of forgiveness or the way in which Jesus faced death that may have melted the heart of Dismas. The criminals and Jesus were suffering the same agony, but Dismas could see that Jesus handled His pain with strength and power. I think, in the six hours that they suffered together, Dismas realized that this man on the cross next to him was no ordinary man. Hearing the taunts of the crowd and seeing the sign over Jesus' head, Dismas would know why Jesus had been condemned and subjected to crucifixion. He could also see that Jesus was not dying like an ordinary criminal. He could see His goodness and His dependence upon God. He would have heard Him address God as His Father and ask for pardon for those who had crucified Him.

As time passed, Gestas carried on with the crowd who continued to mock Jesus, but I imagine that Dismas had grown silent. Then Dismas opened his mouth and said four things, three of them to Gestas and one to Jesus. First to Gestas, *"Don't you fear God,"* he said, *"since you are under the same sentence?"* (Luke 23:40). The Scriptures tell us in many places that the *"fear of the Lord"* is the beginning of wisdom (Proverbs 9:10; 19:23). On the cross, the realization dawned on Dismas that his life was coming to an end, and soon he would have to face God's judgment. He had faced the judgment of men and was found guilty, how much more so when he stood face to face with God? Dismas knew he wasn't coming down from the cross alive. In that very moment, he began to respect God's authority over his life. This is obvious with his next statement to Gestas, *"We are punished justly, for we are getting what our deeds deserve"* (Luke 23:41). Acknowledgement of our sins, without excuse, is the first step on the road to repentance and salvation. The Bible calls this acknowledgement Godly sorrow, and Godly sorrow leads to repentance. Paul the Apostle wrote: "*Godly sorrow brings repentance that leads to salvation and leaves no regret, but worldly sorrow brings death*" (2 Corinthians 7:10). On his cross Dismas knew the state of his soul and he acknowledged that he was reaping what he had sown. He did not excuse, rationalize or justify his sinful condition. He did not offer any alibi. In fact, he passed sentence on himself. He confessed that he was a sinner and he was now paying the price for breaking the laws of the land and the laws of God.

When a person finally recognises and is willing to face up to their sinful condition, they begin to see the holiness of God. They begin to see the awful distance that separates them from God. That is what must have happened to Dismas. We can surmise this because he then said to Gestas, "*But this man has done nothing wrong*" (Luke 23:41b). He had come to the same sober conclusion that Judas and Pilate had arrived at earlier. Judas returned the thirty pieces of silver and said, "*I have sinned, I have betrayed innocent blood*" (Matthew 27:4). Pilate, even though he had sentenced Jesus to die, also publicly acknowledged Jesus' innocence (Matthew 27:24). Even Pilate's wife tried to influence him by sending him a message in the middle of the trial. While Pilate was sitting on the judge's seat, his wife sent him this message: "*Don't have anything to do with that innocent man, for I have suffered a great deal today in a dream because of him*" (Matthew 27:19). When Dismas spoke those words to Gestas, he, by inference, condemned Pilate for his cowardice, and the whole nation of Israel, especially its leaders, for handing Jesus over to be crucified.

In the midst of his agony, Dismas could see the love and compassion of the dying Saviour. Instead of judgment and a thirst for vengeance, there was only mercy and forgiveness. That is when Dismas turned to Jesus and said, "*Jesus, remember me when you come into your kingdom*" (Luke 23:42). This profession of faith is one of the most astonishing events recorded in all of Scripture. The sign above His head said, *This is the King of the Jews,* but Jesus did not resemble any king that we have ever seen. Instead of sitting on a regal throne; He hung from a cross. No majestic crown adorned His head; His brow was pierced with a crown of thorns. Not one servant waited to be beckoned by His hand. Instead, those royal hands and feet were pierced with nails. Outwardly, it looked as if Jesus had no power to save anyone. His enemies had triumphed over Him. His friends were gone and no prophet was standing at the foot of the cross proclaiming, *"Behold, the Lamb of God who takes away the sins of the world"* (John 1:29). Jesus looked like a dying man and nothing else. Nevertheless, through eyes of faith, Dismas saw this suffering, bleeding, dying man as his King and he wanted to be part of his kingdom. Luke tells how Jesus had complimented the faith of the centurion by saying, *"I tell you, I have not found such great faith even in Israel"* (Luke 7:9). Jesus could now say the same thing about Dismas.

We need to remember that this conversion took place before the other miraculous happenings of the day. It happened before the three hours of darkness (Luke 23:44-45). It happened before the curtain of the temple was split from top to bottom (Matthew 27:51). It happened before the earthquake (Matthew 27:51). This man embraced salvation under the most unfavourable conditions possible. He believed and he called out to the one person who had the power to save him. Michael Card in his book, *A Violent Grace,* writes:

> With these words, an unnamed thief becomes the only one we know of to speak to Jesus on the cross without derision or mockery. An unnamed thief is the only person in the Bible who calls Jesus by his personal name, without any kind of title attached, as if their mutual suffering has placed them on an intimate, first-name basis. In so doing, he becomes the first to address Jesus the way most of us do today. And with his words that unnamed thief becomes the first to be drawn to the crucified Christ.[2]

THE CROSS OF RECEPTION

It has been suggested that this criminal used an expression that was a common Jewish form of farewell: "Remember me! Remember me!" In the original Greek, however, his words are actually a *repeated* cry of "Remember me," showing Dismas' desperate need and the urgency of his appeal.[3] He is saying, "Jesus, remember me... Jesus, remember me... Jesus, remember me..."

Jesus responded to this thief with a promise for the future, *"I tell you the truth, today you will be with me in paradise"* (Luke 23:43).

THE JOYS OF RECEPTION

If we were honest with ourselves, most of us would admit we find the story of Dismas unfair. How can someone who has lived a life of depraved indifference to God be offered a place in the kingdom of God? Is that justice? Or is it only what the Lutheran Pastor Dietrich Bonhoeffer described as "cheap grace"? Shouldn't we regard with skepticism the "death-bed" confession of criminals who suddenly, after a full life of crime, "see the light"? It just doesn't seem fair, right or just. So why did Jesus promise this criminal a place in His kingdom? I think He did so to teach about God's amazing gift of love. Let me share with you the joys of reception, the gifts of grace and the biblical truths that can be gleaned from the Cross of Reception.

When we realize that salvation is a free gift from the hand of God, we understand one of the joys of reception. Most of us think that we have to "earn" or "merit" our way into God's kingdom. This conversion story from Calvary Hill shows that can't be true or this thief would have been shut out. He was neither baptized, nor confirmed; he did not take part in the Lord's Supper; he did not perform any good deeds; yet he was the first one through when the gates of paradise were opened. Why? Because salvation is first and foremost about God's amazing *grace*. Down through the years *grace* has been described as "God's unmerited favour." In other words, we do not and cannot earn or ever merit salvation. God grants salvation because He is a compassionate and merciful God. We will not stand before God someday and boast about our accomplishments in this life. We will not give God a list of our good deeds. We will be in the presence of God *only* because of the sacrifice of His Son on the cross. We will be there because His Son took our sin and death upon Himself. He suffered in our place. His blood was shed for our sins, and it is only because of Jesus' sacrifice that we are even able to be in God's presence.

Paul put it this way when writing to the Church in Ephesus: *"For it is by grace you have been saved, through faith—and this not from yourselves, it is the gift of God—not by works, so that no one can boast"* (Ephesians 2:8-9). In many ways, we should not be astounded or offended by this story in Luke's Gospel. Jesus was the "friend of sinners" and it is sinners more than anyone else who need the grace of God. Dismas had a need for grace, and Jesus was able to meet that need.

Helmut Thielicke wrote:

> Jesus gained the power to love harlots, bullies and ruffians...he was able to do this because he saw through the filth and crust of degeneration, because his eye caught the divine original which is hidden in every way—in *every* man...First and foremost he gives us new eyes...When Jesus loved a guilt-laden person and helped him, he saw in him an erring child of God. He saw in him a human being whom his Father loved and grieved over because he was going wrong. He saw him as God originally designed and meant him to be, and therefore he saw through the surface layer of grime and dirt to the real man underneath. Jesus did not *identify* the person with his sin, but rather saw in this sin something alien, something that really did not belong to him, something that merely chained and mastered him and from which he would free him and bring him back to his real self. Jesus was able to love men because he loved them right through the layer of mud.[4]

Although in the eyes of the law Dismas was a convicted criminal, in the eyes of God he was a dying sinner desperately needing redemption. In some ways Dismas' character and plight remind me of John Newton. John Newton was a slave trader who lived in the dark depths of sin; however, a violent storm at sea was the turning point in his life. Motherless at six, and sent to sea on his eleventh birthday, he soon became a teenage dissident. He was forced to join the navy and ended up being flogged for desertion. In time, Newton got himself involved with the African slave trade. In March 1748, at the age of twenty-three, he was on board a cargo ship which was fighting for its life against heavy seas and rough weather. Worn out with pumping and almost frozen, he called out for God's mercy at the height of the storm and was amazed to be saved from certain death. Eventually, Newton renounced his involvement with slave trading and at age thirty-nine, he became a minister in the church. Newton was so amazed that he had experienced first-hand the abundant grace of God, in gratitude he wrote one of the church's greatest hymns, "Amazing Grace," a hymn that's been a blessing for so many for over two hundred years.

> Amazing grace, how sweet the sound
> that saved a wretch like me. I once was lost
> but now I'm found,
> was blind, but now I see.[5]

Like John Newton, Dismas was a wretch who experienced first hand the amazing grace of a merciful and loving God.

When we accept that in some ways Dismas represents all of us, we understand more about the joys of reception. Down through the centuries, Dismas has been referred to as "the good thief." But when you read the Gospel story, there is no evidence of goodness in Dismas. There was no obvious difference between the two criminals before they were crucified. They were very much alike in conduct and in the paths that they had chosen. They were notorious criminals and punished justly by the law for their crimes. The Evangelists reveal that in the beginning, they *both* mocked Jesus. The truth of the matter is—that same spirit of depravity resides in each one of us. You may find that shocking and may protest by saying, "it isn't so," but the Scriptures tell us that, unless we are recipients of divine grace our hearts are no different than the hearts of these two criminals. The prophet Jeremiah wrote: "*The heart is deceitful above all things and beyond cure. Who can understand it?*" (Jeremiah 17:9). Jeremiah's statement has universal implications. It describes what every human heart is by natural birth. Our hearts are deceitful and our minds are at enmity against God. Paul wrote: "*The sinful mind is hostile to God. It does not submit to God's law, nor can it do so. Those controlled by the sinful nature cannot please God*" (Romans 8:7-8). If that is not clear enough, Paul also wrote: "*For all have sinned and fall short of the glory of God*" (Romans 3:23). This is the inheritance of every descendant of Adam. That is what I mean when I say that Dismas is representative of all of us. Like Dismas, we have to come to that place where we admit our guilt and our need for God's grace in our lives.

We are deceived or badly mistaken if we think that we have something to offer God in order to merit this gift of salvation. No, it is not until we see the sickness and corruption within ourselves that we even understand our need for Jesus. Until then, we rely upon our own righteousness, a righteousness that the prophet Isaiah describes as "filthy rags": "*All of us have become like one who is unclean, and all our righteous acts are like filthy rags; we all shrivel up like a leaf, and like the wind our sins sweep us away*" (Isaiah 64:6). We have to let go of the clothes of our own self-righteousness before we can put on God's garments of salvation. We have to admit that we are lost in sin and mischief before we can taste that gift. Some will have to journey quite a distance before they will admit that they are similar to these two criminals or thieves on their crosses. Most will protest and say that they are not criminals or thieves. We might be willing to admit that we are not perfect and may be sinners, but we don't want to be in the same category as these two hanging on the cross. But we are. God has given us the gift of life. He has endowed each of us with special gifts and talents to be used for the glory of God. He has blessed us with memory, reason and skill. He has provided for all our needs. What does He ask for in return? He asks us to give Him our lives. As proof of this we are commanded to: *"Love the Lord your God with all your heart and with all your soul and with all your strength and with all your mind; and, Love your neighbour as yourself"* (Luke 10:27). When we hold ourselves back from God, we are acting like thieves, denying God His rightful place in our lives. For the most part, all that God has given to us has been misappropriated. We have all at one time or another served other masters, whether those masters be the world, the flesh or the devil. Most, if not all of us, have robbed God of what is rightfully His.

Dismas is a sample of what we are by nature and practice. But Dismas recognized how lost he was. He knew that his situation was beyond human repair. He would die in his sin and come face to face with God. So by grace he looked beyond himself to the only One who could save him. *"Jesus, remember me…"* Through the eyes of faith, Dismas was able to see that Jesus hung on that cross because of him. The Godly was suffering for the ungodly and Dismas was the first recipient of the mysterious grace and mercy of God. Paul wrote: *"You see, at just the right time, while we were still powerless, Christ died for the ungodly"* (Romans 5:6). Before any of us can truly taste the goodness of God's salvation, we must come to a place of realized weakness and helplessness. Dismas was nailed to the cross. He would never walk in paths of righteousness on this earth. He could never use his hands to be helping hands for others. He didn't have time to turn over a new leaf or to make any new resolutions. He was dying and all he could do was place his life in the hands of Jesus. He had nothing to offer Jesus but himself.

Are we any different? Is there anything that we can give to God except our lostness? Jesus Christ came into the world to save sinners like Dismas, and we are no different than he was. Paul in writing to Titus put it like this:

> At one time we too were foolish, disobedient, deceived and enslaved by all kinds of passions and pleasures. We lived in malice and envy, being hated and hating one another. But when the kindness and love of God our Saviour appeared, he saved us not because of righteous things we had done, but because of his mercy. He saved us through the washing of rebirth and renewal by the Holy Spirit, whom he poured out on us generously through Jesus Christ our Saviour, so that, having been justified by his grace, we might become heirs having the hope of eternal life. (Titus 3:3-7)

Yes, the grace of God saved Dismas, but he was also an active participant in what took place on the cross. He had to admit his need and he did so to his partner in crime, *"Don't you fear God,' he said, 'since you are under the same sentence? We are punished justly, for we are getting what our deeds deserve.'"* What Dismas offered to Jesus was his repentance. Repentance in many ways is judging ourselves and owning up to the fact that we are lost. When we come to that place, it is not a place of listing our excuses or the extenuating circumstances of our lostness. It's the acknowledgment without excuse of our lostness.

Luke tells the moving parable of the prodigal son. This son asked his father for his inheritance and went off and squandered it in riotous living. When he had spent all he had, he hired himself out to work in a pigpen. While in the pigpen, the parable says, he came to his senses and decided to go home to his father. But he didn't want to come back empty handed and so he made up his confession. He said, *"I will set out and go back to my father and say to him: Father, I have sinned against heaven and against you. I am no longer worthy to be called your son; make me like one of your hired men"* (Luke 15:18). He wanted to offer something to his father for his failure. In some ways, he wanted his father to punish him by making him a hired helper. When the father saw him coming down the road to the house, he ran out and greeted him. The son had time to get only part of his confession out, but his father was not really listening. Instead he poured out his lavish love on this son that had been lost. The father dressed the lost son in a fine robe, put a ring on his finger, sandals on his feet, killed the fattened calf and hosted a party to celebrate his son's return. In this parable, as in the other two parables in Luke chapter 15, Jesus wants His listeners to understand the compassion and mercy of God. In the parable of the lost sheep, Jesus says, *"I tell you that in the same way there will be more rejoicing in heaven over one sinner who repents than over ninety-nine righteous persons who do not need to repent"* (Luke 15:7).

What Jesus suggested in the parable of the prodigal son was scandalous to the Pharisees and the teachers of the law who heard Him giving this teaching. What Jesus gave to this criminal on the cross in many ways is also scandalous. What did he offer to Jesus? All he had to offer was his admittance of guilt. *"We are punished justly, for we are getting what our deeds deserve."* For many of us, that is the hardest thing to admit. Why? Because normally we compare ourselves to others to determine how we measure up. As I said earlier, people have called Dismas the "good thief" because he was repentant. They compare him to Gestas who was unrepentant. But when you compare Dismas and Gestas to the crucified Jesus, neither was good and both were notorious sinners in need of redemption. God's gift of salvation is offered to and received by those who are ready to take their place before God as sinners. Sinners are those who are willing to admit to themselves and to God that they are lost and are in need of redemption. What is it that God gives to those who come to him in this state?

THE GIFTS OF GRACE

From the story of Dismas we learn that there are three gifts of grace that God gives to those who earnestly seek Him and desire to be in right relationship with Him. Outwardly nothing had changed for Dismas. He was still a dying criminal on a cross. Although he had been restored to God, Jesus did not alter his outward circumstances. He suffered through a horrible and agonizing death. Blood streamed down from the wounds in his hands and his feet and he gasped for each breath. Inwardly however, everything had changed for Dismas, for the Scriptures tell us that with the joy of salvation come treasures beyond measure.

God gives to those who come to Him, a gift of faith. Dismas looked at the sign above Jesus' head and by faith knew in his heart that Jesus was indeed a king. This truth is reflected in Dismas' prayer, *"Jesus, remember me when you come into your kingdom."* Most people's faith fluctuates with their feelings. But that is not true faith. The writer to the Hebrews gives us two basic definitions of faith: *"Now faith is being sure of what we hope for and certain of what we do not see."* (Hebrews 11:1). Dismas could not see a kingdom or even a king on the cross next to him, but by faith he believed that Jesus was a king and the head of a kingdom. Hebrews goes on to say: *"And without faith it is impossible to please God, because anyone who comes to him, must believe that he exists and he rewards those who earnestly seek him"* (Hebrews 11: 6). Dismas acknowledged the kingship of Jesus and Jesus promised him paradise. Dismas' revelation was similar to that of the Apostle Peter at Caesarea Philippi.

When Jesus came to the region of Caesarea Philippi, he asked his disciples, "Who do people say the Son of Man is?" They replied, "Some say John the Baptist; others say Elijah; and still others, Jeremiah or one of the prophets." "But what about you?" he asked. "Who do you say I am?" Simon Peter answered, "You are the Christ, the Son of the living God." Jesus replied, "Blessed are you, Simon son of Jonah, for this was not revealed to you by man, but by my Father in heaven." (Matthew 16:13-17)

Neither Peter nor Dismas could take any personal credit, for their revelations came to them from God the Father.

The absolute assurance of God's forgiveness is the second gift we receive. God doesn't hold grudges nor does He keep a little black book with a list of our sins. No, Jesus came to set us free from sin and again and again the Scriptures emphasize that truth. We know that Dismas was a degenerate sinner with a total disregard for the laws of man and God. When he saw the light, he had no difficulty confessing his guilt. So what does God do with our guilt and our sins? The Prophet Isaiah says of those who turn to God: *"'Come now, let us reason together,' says the LORD. 'Though your sins are like scarlet, they shall be as white as snow; though they are red as crimson, they shall be like wool.'"* (Isaiah 1:18). The Psalmist said: *"For as high as the heavens are above the earth, so great is his love for those who fear him; as far as the east is from the west, so far has he removed our transgressions from us. As a father has compassion on his children, so the LORD has compassion on those who fear him; for he knows how we are formed, he remembers that we are dust"* (Psalms 103:11-14). Not only does God remove and forgive our sins, He promises that He will remember them no more. Only God has the kind of power to forget the very offences that we have committed against Him. Isaiah wrote, *"I, even I, am he who blots out your transgressions, for my own sake, and remembers your sins no more"* (Isaiah 43:25). John the Apostle left us two wonderful promises that assure us that sins, no matter what they are, can be completely forgiven: *"If we claim to be without sin, we deceive ourselves and the truth is not in us. If we confess our sins, he is faithful and just and will forgive us our sins and purify us from all unrighteousness"* (1 John 1:8-9). Furthermore, *"But if anybody does sin, we have one who speaks to the Father in our defence—Jesus Christ, the Righteous One. He is the atoning sacrifice for our sins, and not only for ours but also for the sins of the whole world"* (1 John 2:1-2).

As a pastor, it has been my experience that many Christians suffer from unnecessary guilt and self-condemnation, because they do not know that they have been totally forgiven. Some who suffer this way may have an inkling of God's mercy, but they do not realize fully that their sins have been completely blotted out and are remembered no more. None of us is ever excluded from the infinite mercy of Jesus, however great our iniquities. The Scriptures are very clear. If you believe in Jesus, He will save you from your sins. You will notice in the story of Dismas how quickly Jesus assured him of pardon, by promising him a place in His kingdom. More than anything else God is interested in our hearts.

Thank God that the Bible includes all the stories of the giants of faith. King David was one of those giants. But he committed adultery and then tried to cover up that sin, by committing murder. When his sin was discovered, he was without excuse and to his credit he did not try to cover up his sin. He immediately took responsibility for what he had done. Psalm 51 is a beautiful psalm of repentance and acknowledgement of sin. David wrote: *"Against you, you only, have I sinned and done what is evil in your sight, so that you are proved right when you speak and justified when you judge…the sacrifices of God are a broken spirit; a broken and contrite heart, O God, you will not despise"* (Psalms 51:4,17). Although Bathsheba and Uriah were also sinned against, David acknowledged that his primary offence was against God. Although our sins hurt us and others, they cause the most offence to God. What does God require of us? David gives us the answer in *"a broken and contrite heart."* An admittance of guilt restores us to right relationship with God. There is nothing that we can offer to God, but our guilt. A former Archbishop of Canterbury, William Temple, put it like this: "The only thing of my very own which I contribute to my redemption is the sin from which I need to be redeemed."[6] Like the father in the story of the prodigal son, God is there to embrace us and welcome us home. When we repent and then embrace God's plan of redemption, we will receive His gift of forgiveness for the sins we have committed.

The third gift Jesus promised Dismas was paradise or the gift of eternal life. This was not because he deserved it, but because God is love, and Dismas had laid hold of God's love by faith. He did this by reaching out to Jesus. I am sure that he did not understand God's plan of salvation, nor did he understand that on the centre cross, Jesus was taking Dismas' own sin and death on Himself. From that mustard seed of faith, Jesus gave to Dismas much more than he asked. For Dismas to commit his destiny into the hands of One who was, to all outward appearances, unable to save his own life, was a notable achievement of faith and trust. Faith and trust are the essence of salvation. Salvation consists of the union of a sinner with the One who has the power to redeem sinners. Dismas had only a few hours to live and they would be very painful hours, but this criminal had a promise within his heart—a hope for the future. He had entrusted his future into the hands of a king. He knew now that he would live forever in the kingdom that Jesus would establish.

As a pastor, I officiate at many funerals. I begin most funerals by reminding those who have come to bid a final farewell to a loved one, that "death does not have the final say." That is what Jesus said to Dismas, *"Today, you shall be with me in paradise."* There are many questions about heaven that we will not be able to answer here on earth. However, the Scriptures give us some insight as to what the future holds. Some think that those who die, remain unconscious or stay asleep until the Great Resurrection at the end of the ages; and at that time, we will be reunited with our risen bodies on that Resurrection morning. But that is not what Jesus said to Dismas. He promised Dismas that "today" he would be with Him in paradise. It was afternoon by this time and Jesus was promising that before the day was out, Dismas would be with Him in paradise. In Luke's Gospel he uses the word "today" on eleven different occasions. Luke's use of the word never means the past tense or looking forward to a future day, but means the present day. When the angels came to the Shepherds to tell them about the birth of Jesus, they said: *"Today in the town of David a Saviour has been born to you; he is Christ the Lord"* (2:11; see also Luke 4:21; 5:26; 12:28; 19:9; 22:61). Paul writing to the Church in Corinth is very clear that after death believers are with the risen Lord: *"Therefore we are always confident and know that as long as we are at home in the body we are away from the Lord. We live by faith, not by sight. We are confident, I say, and would prefer to be away from the body and at home with the Lord"* (2 Corinthians 5:6-8). The Christian faith teaches that Christians should be ready to face death with complete confidence in the promises of God. As Paul said: *"If only for this life we have hope in Christ, we are to be pitied more than all men"* (1Corinthians 15:19).

When speaking to Dismas Jesus used the word "paradise" which is found in only three verses in the New Testament. Paul spoke of being caught up into paradise. There, he said, he heard inexpressible things; things that man is not permitted to tell. (2 Corinthians 12: 4) In Revelation 2:7, those who overcome will have the right to eat from the tree of life that is in the paradise of God (Revelation 2:7). It is used here by Jesus to describe where Dismas will spend his future. The word "paradise" was a Persian word that came to mean a private park enclosed by some kind of wall, and then, specifically, where a king relaxed with his close friends.[7] In many ways this takes us back to Genesis and the Garden of Eden, where God used to walk with Adam and Eve in the cool of the day (Genesis 3:8). You will find as you read through the Scriptures, however, that "paradise," "heaven" and even the "Garden of Eden" references are used interchangeably and it is truly difficult to distinguish amongst them. What is clear from the Scriptures is that believers will spend eternity in heaven, in paradise or in God's Garden. But what is even more important than the place, is the person *with whom* we will spend eternity. Believers are promised, as Dismas was, that they will be with Jesus in paradise. Heaven without Jesus would not be heaven at all. I think being with the Risen Lord is more important than stories of pearly gates, glittering mansions, streets of gold or choirs of angels. It is to be forever and ever in the presence of Jesus. The night before Jesus left this earth, He said to his apostles, *"Do not let your hearts be troubled. Trust in God; trust also in me. In my Father's house are many rooms; if it were not so, I would have told you. I am going there to prepare a place for you. And if I go and prepare a place for you, I will come back and take you to be with me that you also* may be where I am" (emphasis added) (John 14:1-3). Jesus didn't delegate to others the task of bringing us home; He kept this responsibility for Himself.

I want to finish these reflections on paradise by quoting Richard Hoefler's words from his book *At Noon on Friday.* I believe these words capture the cry of Dismas' heart and the response of the heart of God.

> Is it not enough to know that we shall be remembered by him who made us, planned for us, wept for us, as we stumbled and fell away, emptied himself to come to us, suffered and died for us? Is it not enough to be remembered by such a God, such a Christ, and such a holy Creator-Redeemer? The martyrs and saints of Christendom answer with one voice: 'it is enough. It is enough; to be remembered by God is to be with God, and to be with God is life.' That is what 'remember me' means. It means 'be with me, forsake me not, abide with me!'[8]

THE BIBLICAL TRUTHS

Luke told us this story of Dismas for a number of reasons. Some of the other biblical truths we can learn from these five verses in his Gospel are that the mercy and grace of God are within reach of everyone. We also learn that simple faith is what God wants from us. We are accepted into God's family instantly when we open our hearts to Him, and if we believe in Jesus, we do not die alone.

No one is ever beyond the reach of God's mercy and grace. It is hard to imagine that Dismas, his family and friends could see any hope for a man who chose or fell into a life of crime and mischief. Dismas, along with everyone else, may have given up, but the Father never gives up. In John's Gospel, Jesus told Nicodemus that when He was lifted up, He would draw people to Himself (John 3:14). As

Jesus was lifted up from the earth on that Cross of Redemption, He drew Dismas to Himself—and thus began fulfilling the promise He had made to Nicodemus.

These verses teach us the truth that God wants and accepts simple faith from us. In Matthew's Gospel, Jesus told us that those who would like to be great in the kingdom of God must become like little children. *"I tell you the truth, unless you change and become like little children, you will never enter the kingdom of Heaven. Therefore, whoever humbles himself like this child is the greatest in the kingdom of Heaven"* (Matthew 18:2-4). Dismas was helpless, hopeless, lost, forsaken, guilty under the law, condemned to die by crucifixion, but the cry of his heart was the cry of a child, *"Remember me..."* That humble cry reached the heart of Jesus and He was able to give to Dismas the assurance of eternal salvation. It is unfortunate that at times we have put many barriers or obstacles in front of those who are seeking a genuine relationship with God. We have to accept that the message of salvation is not a complicated one. Paul described how easy it was:

> *That if you confess with your mouth, "Jesus is Lord" and believe in your heart that God raised him from the dead; you will be saved. For it is with your heart that you believe and are justified, and it is with your mouth that you confess and are saved...anyone who trusts in him, will never be put to shame...everyone who calls on the name of Lord will be saved.* (Romans 10:9-13)

When the Scriptures say anyone, we can be assured that it means anyone or everyone!

We should not doubt the truth of our instant acceptance into God's family when we open our hearts to Him. Paul said:

> *For you did not receive a spirit that makes you a slave again to fear, but you received the Spirit of sonship. And by him we cry, "Abba, Father." The Spirit himself testifies with our spirit that we are God's children. Now if we are children, then we are heirs—heirs of God and co-heirs with Christ.* (Romans 8:15-17)

THE CROSS OF RECEPTION

To the Church in Ephesus, Paul wrote:

For he chose us in him before the creation of the world to be holy and blameless in his sight. In love he predestined us to be adopted as his children through Jesus Christ, in accordance with his pleasure and will to the praise of his glorious grace, which he has freely given us in the One he loves. In him we have redemption through his blood, the forgiveness of sins, in accordance with the riches of God's grace that he lavished on us with all wisdom and understanding. (Ephesians 1:3-8)

When Dismas turned to Christ, he was forgiven immediately, accepted into the family of God and promised an eternal place in heaven. Some, as I said earlier, may think that kind of grace is unfair. We need to remember however, that the Cross of Redemption puts *all* human beings on the same level. It reminds us that we have *all* sinned. It may be that our sins are not as grave as the sins of Dismas, but we all need the same redemption that he received. At their death who would not want to receive the kind of mercy and grace that Jesus extended to this criminal? We may think that we are not serious sinners, but with God there are no little sins, *there are only sins.*

It is a truth that those who know Jesus do not die alone. I turn again to the words of Richard Hoefler.

The sting of death, any death, is the loneliness of dying, the sense of facing the unknown alone; this is the terrifying sting of death. But to die not alone—to die rather in the arms of a friend takes away the sting and gives to death a ringing note of victory—a victory that makes conquerors out of cowards, and enables us to die not as beasts but nobly as beloved children of God. Particularly is this true when the one who has us in his arms—his caring arms—is God incarnate! 'Lord, remember me!' Hold me! Let me not die alone! To the prayer of this thief and to us comes the magnificent promise of Jesus Christ our Lord: 'Today, thou shalt be with me in paradise.' Where paradise is we do not know. But this we do know—paradise is with

55

him! That is the meaning of this second word from the cross. That God will not forget us; in every hour of trial and torment he will surely come! In every moment of need, he will be there! We shall all face death. Like every other creature we shall die; but we die not alone. We die with him, and he dies with us. His death was an act of victory; therefore we share not only in his death but also in his victory and life. 'Yea, though I walk through the valley of the shadow of death, I will fear no evil, for thou art with me.' 'Lord, remember me when thou comest into thy kingdom.' Hold me! Hug me! 'Verily, I say unto thee, today, shalt thou be with me in paradise.'[9]

This story of the repentant thief tells us that we do not have to reach a certain standard of holiness before God will accept us as His children. It tells us that we don't have to get our wayward lives under control before we come to Jesus. It tells us that our salvation is not based on our merit or our many good works, but only upon the grace and tender mercies of our God. In some ways we should not be surprised to find this story in the Gospel of Luke. Jesus had said earlier to the "religious ones" of his day, that the tax collectors and prostitutes would enter the kingdom of God and the self-righteous would be cast out (Matthew 21:31). We need to remember always that it is not the outward appearance that God is interested in, but the heart that beats inwardly, hungering for the things of God. *"Blessed are the poor in spirit; for theirs is the kingdom of God…blessed are those who hunger and thirst for righteousness, for they will be filled…blessed are the pure in heart for they shall see God"* (Matthew 5:3, 6, 8).

On the Cross of Reception, Dismas died to sin. In the blink of an eye, he was changed from a dying sinner into a dying saint. He died with every sin he had ever committed completely blotted out and remembered no more. God's amazing grace and love that were so evident on Calvary Hill two thousand years ago, are available today to every one who reaches out and says: *"Jesus, remember me…Jesus, remember me… Jesus, remember me…."*

CHAPTER 3

THE CROSS OF REJECTION

One of the criminals who hung there hurled insults at him: "Aren't you the Christ? Save yourself and us!" (Luke 23:39)

There are no known churches or fellowship groups named after the criminal Gestas. He has a place in history only because he was crucified on Jesus' left, and he is known as the unrepentant thief or criminal. Luke reports that Gestas spoke only a few words while he was dying next to Jesus: "*One of the criminals who hung there hurled insults at him: 'Aren't you the Christ? Save yourself and us!'*" (Luke 23:39). The text seems to suggest, however, that Gestas kept repeating those words. Usually those who are condemned are drawn together because of their shared misery. The normal practice of those who were sentenced to crucifixion was to strike out at those who had damned them to death.

Throughout His ministry, Jesus was identified as a friend of sinners. There is no record that He was ever insulted by the marginalized or the outcast. Others may have insulted them, but Jesus always identified with them, and they with Him. But on this Good Friday one of the sinners that Jesus came to save railed against Him. The word "railed" means to utter reproaches, to scoff, to use insolent and reproachful language. As this criminal was dying on the cross next to Jesus, he blasphemed the only one who could truly save him. He, like Dismas, could also read the sign above Jesus' head that read: *This is the King of the Jews.* Instead of reaching out to Jesus, he turned and said sarcastically to Him, *"Aren't you the Christ? Save yourself and us!"* (Luke 23:39b). When he heard the others on the ground challenging and taunting Jesus to come down from the cross, he joined his voice with theirs.

Gestas, however, was not concerned about deliverance from sin or eternal salvation. What he was seeking was deliverance from his cross. He knew that he was facing death and he was seeking a way out. This cry of Gestas was not a cry of repentance seeking mercy—it was a cry of unbelief. *"Aren't you the Christ?"* This statement implies, "Well, if you are the Christ, surely you can save yourself and us?" There may have been hope in Gestas' heart that Jesus really was the Messiah and if so, He could step down from that cross, destroy His enemies and set up His kingdom here on earth. When he asked Jesus to save Himself and the two of them, he was not using the word *save* as a plea but as a command. It was the same word that others on the ground were using. *"If you are the king of the Jews,* save *yourself!"* (Luke 23:37, emphasis added). Prove to us that you are the Christ by coming down from the cross! But if He couldn't or wouldn't do that, Gestas wanted no part of Him. He was rejecting the one who could save him, not from the cross, but from eternal death.

Jesus did not respond to Gestas' insults or taunts. Perhaps because of Jesus' silence, Dismas decided to speak to Gestas. Dismas became an evangelist for the cause of Jesus. First, he said to Gestas, *"Don't you fear God, since you are under the same sentence?"* Dismas' emphasis was probably on the word *fear.* When Scripture uses the word fear, it does so in a number of ways. According to the *New Bible Dictionary,* first, there is 'Holy Fear' or reverence for God.

58

This is a healthy fear, for it is a God-given fear enabling people to reverence God's authority, obey His commandments and hate and shun all form of evil. The Old and New Testaments speak of the absolute Sovereignty of God and this Sovereignty contributed to the 'fear of the Lord.' (This is a holy fear that for the most part has been forgotten among today's Christians.) This fear is not to hold people in bondage, but to set them free to walk in humility, acknowledging God as their Sovereign Lord. In the Old Testament, largely because of the law's legal sanctions, true religion was often regarded as synonymous with the fear of God.[1]

For example the Prophet Jeremiah wrote, *"'Your wickedness will punish you; your backsliding will rebuke you. Consider then and realize how evil and bitter it is for you when you forsake the Lord your God and have no awe of me,' declares the Lord, the Lord Almighty"* (Jeremiah 2: 19).

The second fear is a "slavish fear" and is strictly a natural consequence of sin.[2] We see this fear first appearing in Genesis, chapter 3, when God is seeking Adam and Eve. Adam says to God, *"I heard you in the garden, and I was afraid because I was naked; so I hid"* (Genesis 3:10).

A third fear is the "fear of people," and it manifests itself as a kind of a blind dread of what others may do to us.[3] Proverbs and John's first letter tell us how to overcome this fear: *"Fear of man will prove to be a snare, but whoever trusts in the Lord is kept safe"* (Proverbs 29:25). John the Apostle wrote:

If anyone acknowledges that Jesus is the Son of God, God lives in him and he in God. And so we know and rely on the love God has for us. God is love. Whoever lives in love lives in God, and God in him. In this way, love is made complete among us so that we will have confidence on the Day of Judgment, because in this world we are like him. There is no fear in love. But perfect love drives out fear, because fear has to do with punishment. The one who fears is not made perfect in love. (1 John 4:15-18)

Those who are believers in Jesus, have no reason to fear, because they live in Jesus and Jesus lives in them, and the perfect love of God drives out fear. Probably for the first time in his life, Dismas had an appreciation of the "fear of the Lord" and this was the message that he was trying to convey to his fellow-sufferer. Dismas was trying to pierce Gestas' conscience and heart by reminding him that soon they would both face death, and after death stand before God for judgment. In their present condition, they had reason to fear this judgment. In short, "Gestas, why add to your guilt by railing against this innocent man?" Those on the ground could mock Jesus with a feeling of impunity, but not the ones who were dying next to Him. Those on the ground may have had time to genuinely repent of their words and actions, but those who were crucified next to Jesus were facing imminent death and their time was close at hand.

The second part of the story of the two criminals who died next to Jesus is sad and tragic. There is no indication from the Scriptures that Gestas ever acknowledged the innocence of Jesus or his own guilt. We never hear of Gestas repenting of his sins or even making an effort to reach out for Jesus. He had the same opportunity as Dismas, but he chose to rail against Jesus instead of seeking His mercy and forgiveness. He wanted a victorious king, not the king dying next to him who was condemned as a common criminal.

Although Gestas' ending is tragic, there are lessons for us to learn from this unrepentant thief. As Dismas is representative of each of us, so too is Gestas. One criminal chose life and the other chose death. These are also the choices we face. When people speak of God's gifts to humanity, the "love of God" is rightly treasured above all other gifts. Most people are familiar with this well known verse of Scripture: *"For God so loved the world, that he gave his one and only Son, that whoever believes in him shall not perish but have eternal life"* (John 3:16). Yes, God loves this world and each individual in ways that are indescribable. No writer could put into words how awesome and all encompassing is God's love for each one of us.

In conjunction with this love however, God also grants to us the awesome gift of *free choice*. If you read the above verse of Scripture carefully, you will note that it says, "whoever believes." That is the choice we *all* have to make. God always honours this gift of free choice that He has generously granted to humanity. Every covenant agreement entered into by God and humanity had two sides. At no time do we read of God 'forcing' His will on His creation. In the very first covenant, Adam and Eve were placed in the Garden of Eden and God instructed them not to eat of the tree of the knowledge of good and evil. They chose to disobey and rebel against God's command. When Jesus came to the people of Israel to share with them God's Good News of salvation, apart from a handful of disciples, the people and their leaders chose to reject Him, and to crucify God's messenger. As there were consequences for Adam and Eve, so there are consequences for those who by their own free will choose to reject the sacrificial death of Jesus on the Cross of Redemption. Dismas chose to reach out to Jesus, while Gestas did not.

Gestas chose in the last hours of his life to rail against Jesus and to turn away from Him. Why do people reject Jesus and what are the consequences of such a rejection? These consequences are as applicable today as they were two thousand years ago.

WHY JESUS IS REJECTED

Gestas' attitude to Jesus shows us that not everyone will accept Jesus Christ as the Son of the Living God. Not all will accept that He came into this world to die for sinners. Over the years, I have found many who objected to Jesus. Although the excuses are varied, I have discovered in general that there are three primary reasons why people would reject so great a salvation. Of course, people's rejection of Jesus is not limited to these three, but I have found that they are the most common.

1) The belief that Jesus Christ is not the only way to God

The most popular reason for the rejection of Jesus is the modern day belief that all religions lead to God and it does not matter which god you choose to follow. Since the launching of the Hubble Space Telescope, scientists tell us that our universe is expanding.[4] That may be true, but the world in which we now live is shrinking. World population has grown to over six billion people.[5] As a result, we have become a "Global Village." Immigrants from every nation in the world now mingle with those whose roots are in the Western world. With these immigrants, came many religions. People have come to believe and to insist that one religion is the same as another and eventually all will lead to God. That kind of thinking is very tolerant, and in our world, tolerance is almost viewed as the Eleventh Commandment. So the order of the day is that every person can create his or her own definition of truth. But how is it possible that all religions lead to God when each is so different from the other? Most people who object to Jesus and the claims of Christianity generally have not seriously examined the major world religions and what they say about God, personal salvation and an after life. This is not the place to explore each one in depth, but it is foolish to think and believe that they all point in the same direction. Each of them views God, salvation and eternity in very different ways and the differences are irreconcilable.

Christians believe and worship one God in Trinity and the Trinity in Unity as the Father, Son and Holy Spirit. All the claims of Christianity rest on the completed work of the Lord Jesus Christ, who was empowered by the Holy Spirit and sent by the Father into this world to die for sinners: "*Salvation is found in no one else, for there is no other name under heaven given to men, by which we must be saved*" (Acts 4:12). As for eternity, the last book of the Bible describes it this way:

Then I saw a new heaven and a new earth, for the first heaven and the first earth had passed away, and there was no longer any sea. I

THE CROSS OF REJECTION

saw the Holy City, the New Jerusalem, coming down out of heaven from God, prepared as a bride beautifully dressed for her husband. And I heard a loud voice from the throne saying, "Now the dwelling of God is with men, and he will live with them. They will be his people, and God himself will be with them and be their God. He will wipe every tear from their eyes. There will be no more death or mourning or crying or pain, for the old order of things has passed away." (Revelation 21:1-4)

Christians believe and teach that Jesus Christ said, *"I am the way and the truth and the life. No one comes to the Father except through me"* (John 14:6). Many people of other faiths or no faith at all find this claim arrogant and offensive. Some believe and teach that Jesus' statement in John chapter 14 must be in error. Either John the Apostle was mistaken when he wrote those words or else Jesus was badly misguided about being the only way to God. From the earliest description by God of who He is—His conversation with Moses—we find Him describing Himself as simply, "**I am.**" It is no coincidence that Jesus used the same expression in His pivotal statements. In effect He was saying, "God is…" When Jesus said, "**I am** the Way…", it was only one of ten such statements to be found in the Gospel of John and in the book of Revelation.

*Then Jesus declared, "**I am** the bread of life. He who comes to me will never go hungry, and he who believes in me will never be thirsty."* (John 6:35)

*"I tell you the truth," Jesus answered, "before Abraham was born, **I am!**"* (John 8:58)

*"While I am in the world, **I am** the light of the world."* (John 9:5)

*Jesus said again, "I tell you the truth, **I am** the gate for the sheep."* (John 10:7)

"I am the good shepherd. The good shepherd lays down his life for the sheep." (John 10:11)

Jesus said, "I am the resurrection and the life. He who believes in me will live, even though he dies." (John 11:25)

"I am the vine; you are the branches. If a man remains in me and I in him, he will bear much fruit; apart from me you can do nothing." (John 15:5)

"I am the Alpha and the Omega," says the Lord God, "who is, and who was, and who is to come, the Almighty." (Revelation 1:8)

When I saw him, I fell at his feet as though dead. Then he placed his right hand on me and said: "Do not be afraid. I am the First and the Last." (Revelation 1:17)

What do we make of all of these claims? Do we dismiss them or say that the writers misinterpreted what Jesus said? No one said it better than C.S. Lewis in his book, *Mere Christianity.*

People often say about Jesus: 'I'm ready to accept Jesus as a great moral teacher, but I don't accept His claim to be God.' That is the one thing we must not say. A man who was merely a man and said the sort of things Jesus said would not be a great moral teacher. He would either be a lunatic—on a level with the man who says he is a poached egg—or else he would be the Devil of Hell. You must make your choice. Either this man was, and is, the Son of God, or else a madman or something worse. You can shut Him up for a fool, you can spit at Him and kill Him as a demon; or you can fall at His feet and call Him Lord and God. But let us not come with any patronizing nonsense about His being a great human teacher. He has not left that open to us. He did not intend to.[6]

If one does a careful examination of world religions, it should not be difficult to see that the religion offering the most hope is Christianity. According to the basic teaching of Christianity, God sent His Son into the world to save us and to reconcile us to Him. The teachings of the Scriptures say that no one can save or make him- or herself right with God. There is uniqueness to the Christian claims that cannot be ignored or dismissed. Christians claim that God has intervened in history. As human beings we could not reach or climb our way up to God, so God came down to us. He didn't come as a conquering hero or a God-like figure; as the Apostle Paul put it, He came as a servant to show us the way to God:

> *Who (Jesus), being in very nature God, did not consider equality with God something to be grasped, but made himself nothing, taking the very nature of a servant, being made in human likeness. And being found in appearance as a man, he humbled himself and became obedient to death-even death on a cross! Therefore God exalted him to the highest place and gave him the name that is above every name, that at the name of Jesus every knee should bow, in heaven and on earth and under the earth, and every tongue confess that Jesus Christ is Lord, to the glory of God the Father.* (Philippians 2:6-11)

These are the Christian claims.

Please understand that I do not casually dismiss the other religions of the world, as there is truth, goodness and morality to be found in each of them. What separates Christianity from each of them is the absolute belief that Jesus Christ came into this world *to die for the sins* of humanity and to set each person right with God. The other religions of the world do not tell you about a God who loves you enough to reveal Himself to you so that you can be reconciled and made right. Neither do they offer you a "grace-filled" God, who bled and died to remove the barriers between God and humanity. This God who was crucified, died and buried did not stay in the grave. He rose from the grave to show us that sin and death have been removed.

Although people may say that they stumble over Jesus, they have to concede that they stumble over a Jesus who rose victoriously over death (see Chapter 5).

2) Stumbling Over The Cross

A second reason given for rejecting Jesus is the cross itself. From the earliest time, Christians have claimed that the Cross of Redemption is central to the Christian Faith. Although Dismas could recognize the kingship of Jesus and reach out to embrace Him, Gestas could not. To Gestas it was foolish to believe that the one hanging next to him was really the *King of the Jews*. That unbelief has carried down through the corridors of time and today many simply dismiss the cross. To show that the cross is central and key to reconciliation with God, we have to look at what has been said about the cross, and we will start with what Jesus said about His cross.

> *"I am the good shepherd; I know my sheep and my sheep know me—just as the Father knows me and I know the Father—and I lay down my life for the sheep...the reason my Father loves me is that I lay down my life—only to take it up again. No one takes it from me, but I lay it down of my own accord. I have authority to lay it down and authority to take it up again. This command I received from my Father."* (John 10:14-15, 17-18)

> *"Just as Moses lifted up the snake in the desert, so the Son of Man must be lifted up, that everyone who believes in him may have eternal life."* (John 3:14)

> *"For even the Son of Man did not come to be served, but to serve, and to give his life as a ransom for many."* (Mark 10:45) (See Cross of Redemption for a clear understanding of Christ's suffering and death.)

THE CROSS OF REJECTION

What did Jesus' followers have to say about the cross? None of the writers of the New Testament shied away from the fact that Jesus the Messiah was crucified:

"Therefore let all Israel be assured of this: God has made this Jesus, whom you crucified, both Lord and Christ." (Acts 2:36)

"Then know this, you and all the people of Israel: It is by the name of Jesus Christ of Nazareth, whom you crucified but whom God raised from the dead…He is 'the stone you builders rejected, which has become the capstone.'" (Acts 4:10-11)

"I have been crucified with Christ and I no longer live, but Christ lives in me. The life I live in the body, I live by faith in the Son of God, who loved me and gave himself for me." (Galatians 2:20)

"Unlike the other high priests, he does not need to offer sacrifices day after day, first for his own sins. And then for the sins of the people. He sacrificed for their sins once for all when he offered himself." (Hebrews 7:27).

"When you were dead in your sins and in the uncircumcision of your sinful nature, God made you alive with Christ. He forgave us all our sins, having cancelled the written code, with its regulations, that was against us and that stood opposed to us; he took it away, nailing it to the cross." (Colossians 2:13-15)

"He himself bore our sins in his body on the tree, so that we might die to sins and live for righteousness; by his wounds you have been healed." (1 Peter 2:24)

This is what some of the giants of the Christian faith have expressed about Jesus and His cross down through the ages:

The Swiss theologian, Emil Brunner, wrote:

The cross is the sign of the Christian faith, of the Christian Church, of the revelation of God in Jesus Christ...The whole struggle of the Reformation for the *sola fide,* the *soli deo gloria,* was simply the struggle for the right interpretation of the Cross. He who understands the Cross aright—this is the opinion of the Reformers—understands the Bible, he understands Jesus Christ. [7]

The evangelical writer and scholar, John Stott, in his book *The Cross of Christ* wrote:

For the cross is at the centre of the evangelical faith... It lies at the centre of the historic biblical faith. It gives us a new, worshipping relationship to God, a new and balanced understanding of ourselves, a new incentive to give ourselves in mission, a new love for our enemies and a new courage to face the perplexities of suffering. [8]

The Anglican theologian, J.I. Packer, says: "The cross is central... and it takes us to the very heart of the Christian Gospel."[9]

P. T. Forsyth, the English Congregationalist, in *The Cruciality of the Cross,* wrote: "Christ is to us just what his cross is. All that Christ was in heaven or on earth was put into what he did there...Christ, I repeat, is to us just what his cross is. You do not understand Christ till you understand his cross." In his book, *The Work of Christ,* he wrote: "On this interpretation of the work of Christ (the Pauline doctrine of reconciliation) the whole Church rests. If you move faith from that centre, you have driven *the* nail into the Church's coffin. The Church is then doomed to death, and it is only a matter of time when she shall expire."[10]

The Anglican scholar, Bishop Stephen Neill, wrote: "In the Christian theology of history, the death of Christ is the central point of history; here all roads of the past converge; hence all the roads of the future diverge."[11]

THE CROSS OF REJECTION

The great scholar and theologian, William Barclay, in his book, *Crucified and Crowned* wrote:

> One thing I know—that because of Jesus Christ and because of what he is and did and does, my whole relationship with God is changed. Because of Jesus Christ I know that God is my father and friend. Daily and hourly I experience the fact that I can enter his presence with confidence and with boldness. He is no longer my enemy; he is no longer even my judge. There is no longer an unbridgeable gulf between him and me. I am more at home with him than with any human being in the world. And all this is so because of Jesus Christ, and it could not possibly have happened without him.[12]

The evangelist and writer, Canon Michael Green, wrote in his book, *The Empty Cross of Jesus*:

> The cross of Jesus is the very core of the gospel, and it needs to be re-examined in every generation. The human heart shrinks from the cross. It is too painful, too bloody, too humiliating for proud modern man. And so we prefer to concentrate on the absence of God, or man come of age, or the Church, or the Holy Spirit. The cross remains for us, as it did for the first century, both 'folly' and a 'stumbling block' and yet it is the power of God and the wisdom of God. The cross is the central symbol in Christian Churches. The cross lies at the heart of the Holy Communion, the only service Jesus left behind Him. The cross is the key to the ultimate problem of how a holy God can accept sinners into His company. So fundamental is the cross of Jesus to Christianity that no apology needs to be offered for further examination of this central mystery of the faith.[13]

Finally, in his book, *The Cross*, the great preacher and minister of Westminster Chapel in London, Martyn Lloyd-Jones, wrote:

> The preaching of the cross, the preaching of the death of the Lord Jesus Christ on that cross is the very heart and centre of

the Christian Gospel and the Christian message … the cross is the centre of the apostolic preaching because it is the thing that saves us. It does not ask us to save ourselves, it does not tell us to do something that will save us, it says it is done, it has happened, it was happening there … any person who is saved, is saved by the cross, and to be saved means that your sins are forgiven, that you are reconciled to God. You have become a child of God, and you begin to receive His blessing. You have no fear of death, or the grace and the judgment. You know that you are going to inherit glory.[14]

The cross that millions wear to identify themselves as Christians might seem to be an odd symbol to some people. After all, the cross was first and foremost an instrument of gruesome torture. Yet two thousand years after the death of the founder of Christianity, the cross remains as the authentic badge of Christianity.

The early Church used the symbol of a fish to identify themselves to one another. "Only the initiated would know, and nobody else could guess, that *ichthys* (fish) was an acronym for *Jesus Christos Theou Huios Soter* (Jesus Christ, Son of God, Saviour). But it did not remain the Christian sign, doubtless because the association between Jesus and a fish was purely acronymic (a fortuitous arrangement of letters) and had no visual significance."[15] The cross did not start to appear in the Church until one hundred and fifty years after the death of Jesus. Why did it take the early Christians that long to start portraying the cross as a Christian symbol? Were they ashamed of or embarrassed by it? No, it is believed that the early Church strongly resisted using the cross as a symbol of their faith because it meant far too much to them. The cross was a reminder of the terrible price that God was willing to pay to secure the salvation of humanity. Admittedly, not all those who now wear the cross, wear it out of allegiance to the crucified Christ. They wear it not as an icon of faith, but as a fashion statement. A well-known female pop singer reportedly said: "It's sexy to wear a crucifix because there is a naked man on it." Her statement reflects a deliberate movement in the secular world to strip the cross of its meaning.

To truly understand all that the cross means we need to consider Paul's words from 1 Corinthians:

> *For the message of the Cross is foolishness to those who are perishing; but to us who are being saved, it is the power of God. For it is written: "I will destroy the wisdom of the wise; the intelligence of the intelligent I will frustrate." Where is the wise man? Where is the Scholar? Where is the philosopher of this age? Has not God made foolish the wisdom of the world? For since in the wisdom of God the world through its wisdom did not know him, God was pleased through the foolishness of what was preached to save those who believe. Jews demand miraculous signs and Greeks look for wisdom, but we preach Christ crucified: a stumbling block to Jews and foolishness to Gentiles, but to those whom God has called, both Jews and Greeks, Christ the power of God and the wisdom of God. For the foolishness of God is wiser than man's wisdom, and the weakness of God is stronger than man's strength. Brothers, think of what you were when you were called. Not many of you were wise by human standards; not many were influential; not many were of noble birth. But God chose the foolish things of the world to shame the wise; God chose the weak things of the world to shame the strong. He chose the lowly things of this world and the despised things—and the things that are not—to nullify the things that are, so that no one may boast before him. It is because of him that you are in Christ Jesus, who has become for us wisdom from God—that is, our righteousness, holiness and redemption. Therefore, as it written: "Let him who boasts, boast in the Lord." (1 Corinthians 1:18-31)*

In this passage Paul declares that the central message of Christianity is the cross of Christ. In verse 18, we are invited to set aside human wisdom and seek the wisdom of God: *"For the message of the cross is foolishness to those who are perishing, but to us who are being saved, it is the power of God."* What were the people of Paul's day seeking? Paul answers in verses 22-23: *"Jews demand miraculous signs and Greeks look for wisdom, but we preach Christ crucified: a stumbling block to Jews and foolishness to Gentiles, but to those whom God has called, both Jews and Greeks, Christ the power of God and the wisdom of God."* Why did the Greek and Jewish people of Paul's day find the cross so offensive? The civilized Greeks were seen as the sophisticated privileged people of the ancient world. They placed their hope in wisdom and they found the preaching of the cross to be foolishness. They could not conceive a God who would come to this earth to suffer and to die. To them it was utter madness. In fact, the whole idea of the incarnation—of God becoming man—was revolting to the Greek mind. For the Greek, one who suffered as Jesus suffered was proof that Jesus could not possibly be the Son of any God. The preacher who came with a blunt message of crucifixion was not to be respected, believed or even listened to.

Paul says that the Jewish people of his day demanded miraculous signs and the cross to them was a stumbling block. It was incredible to the Jewish leaders that one who ended his life upon a cross or a tree could be God's chosen Messiah. Furthermore, they would look upon Jesus as accursed—because anyone who is hung on a tree is under God's curse (Deuteronomy 21:23). The Messiah they were seeking was to be a conquering Messiah, one who would overthrow the Romans and restore Israel to its former glory. When Jesus walked among them, they taunted Him constantly by asking Him *to show them a sign* that He was the long awaited Messiah. The healing of the sick, the raising of the dead, the feeding of the five thousand were not sufficient signs. Messiah to them meant power, splendour and triumph. On the other hand, death on a cross meant weakness, humiliation, defeat and curse. The preaching of the cross was indeed a stumbling block, and also a scandal and an impossible portrayal of God's chosen and anointed one.

So to the Jews and Greeks of Paul's day, the central message of Christianity sounded like pure foolishness or utter madness. Neither could conceive for a moment a God who came into this world and who would claim to die for the sins of the world on a cross. How could any sane person worship as God a dead man who had been condemned as a criminal and subjected to the most humiliating form of execution? The combination of death, crime and shame put Jesus beyond respect, let alone worship.

Two thousand years later, the cross still seems like foolishness to some and many people from all walks of life continue to stumble over Jesus and His cross. Preaching the true message of the cross in the twenty-first century is equally as difficult as it was in the first century. Most people are much more comfortable with a victorious spirituality and when you first glance at the cross, all you see is humiliation and shame. Richard Neuhaus, in his book *Death on a Friday Afternoon*, tells a story that is worth repeating.

> Some while ago I was on the same lecture platform with a famous television evangelist from California who is noted for accenting the positive and upbeat in the Christian message. According to this evangelist, it is as with Coca-Cola: Everything goes better with Jesus. He had built a huge new church called, let us say, New Life Cathedral, and he explained that during the course of the building there was a debate about whether the cathedral should feature a cross. It was thought that the cross might prompt negative thoughts, maybe even thoughts about suffering and death. 'Finally, I said that of course there will be a cross,' the famous evangelist said. 'After all, the cross is the symbol of Christianity and we are a Christian Church. But I can guarantee you,' he declared with a triumphant smile, 'there is nothing downbeat about the cross at New Life Cathedral!'[16]

Like this evangelist, many are scandalized by the truth that Christians worship a "crucified God." Because so many do not like the idea of a crucified God, they have shifted the focus of Christianity from the cross to other aspects of the Christian faith. The favourite for many in the pulpit today is to focus upon Jesus' teaching and example. They say that His teaching far surpasses any other teaching in the world and that Jesus was the greatest religious philosopher who ever lived. They say that what people need to hear today is good teaching on Jesus' discourse on the Mount of Olives. I agree that the Sermon on the Mount is still the greatest sermon ever preached. People are attracted to this teaching for it lays out for them an ethical standard of behaviour and morals. As with the Ten Commandments, however, it is impossible to live up to the demands of this sermon in our own strength and power, because of our inherited sinful nature.

If people don't focus on Jesus' teaching, they tend to focus upon his Godly example. People are encouraged to imitate Jesus, but how do you imitate one who lived a sinless life? Yes, we are called to pay close attention to the teaching of Jesus and have our lives sanctified in holiness. But neither Jesus' teaching, example, wisdom nor miracles were the focus of the preaching of the Apostles. They preached Jesus crucified and the meaning of His death. Paul's great desire in life can be summed up in two passages of Scripture. To the Corinthians he wrote: *"For I resolved to know nothing while I was with you except Jesus Christ and him crucified"* (1 Corinthians 2:2). He wrote to the Church in Galatia: *"May I never boast except in the cross of our Lord Jesus Christ, through which the world has been crucified to me, and I to the world"* (Galatians 6:14). Paul never apologized for preaching the message of the cross, for again and again he told us that it is in the cross where we find life and liberty. Christians are not to regret or to downplay the cross of Jesus. We are not called to idealize it, philosophize about it or turn it into something beautiful, so that it will not cause offence and will be acceptable to all. Without the cross, there would be no Christian Gospel to proclaim. It is the cross that saves humanity, for without the cross we would all be lost and without hope in a world that at times seems to have gone mad with evil and injustice.

3) Evil, Injustice, Suffering and Destruction

The evil, injustice, suffering and destruction in our world are other reasons why many reject Jesus and the message of Christianity. When we look back on the twentieth century, we see a century of war, destruction, unjust suffering, and senseless bloodshed. In this last century, there have been two wars that engulfed most nations. Since the end of the Second World War, there have been almost unending conflicts—in Korea, Vietnam, Afghanistan, Iran and Iraq to name a few. All of these so-called conflicts have resulted in major loss of life, economic hardships and senseless suffering for many innocent people. In this last century we have seen a rise of evil dictators who have left behind them waves of mass destruction. Under Joseph Stalin about 20 million Russian people died of starvation, execution and enforced slavery. Another 20 million suffered imprisonment and deportation. During the reign of Pol Pot in Cambodia, between one and two million Cambodians were massacred. Mao Zedong controlled China from 1949-1976 and subjected the Chinese people to his massive social experiments, all of which went awry. When he launched the Great Leap Forward—his economic plan to forge an industrial revolution in China—it resulted in the worst famine of the century, described as a 'totally unnecessary, man-made holocaust' that claimed between 23 million and 30 million lives. Also during his reign, millions were imprisoned, tortured, and murdered as suspected class enemies. In addition to the man-made wars, destruction and holocausts which have beset the twentieth century, the disease 'AIDS' which emerged in 1981, now runs rampant and seemingly out of control to the four corners of the globe. As the twentieth century drew to a close, some 34.3 million men, women, and children faced a future dominated by a fatal disease unknown just a few decades ago. According to new estimates from the World Health Organization 33 million adults and 1.3 million children were living with HIV by the end of 1999.

On September 11, 2001 two hijacked aircraft crashed into the World Trade Center in New York City killing over two thousand civilians. Many of the victims were fire fighters, paramedics and police officers who were on a rescue mission to free people trapped in the twin office towers. A third aircraft crashed into the Pentagon and a fourth hijacked aircraft crashed in a field in Pennsylvania. The death toll from these major terrorist attacks was close to three thousand people. A bomb exploded in Bali, Indonesia killing close to two hundred people. A sniper loose in the Washington area indiscriminately shot and killed thirteen people. In the Middle East, Israel and Palestine are locked in a seemingly never-ending bloody conflict. In spite of all of our advances in science, medical research, education and social reform, we live in extremely dangerous times.

The cold hand of fear grips many people today, and they ask the age-old question, WHY? Why is there so much destruction and evil in our world? Why do so many bad things happen to good and innocent people? If the God of creation is so wise, powerful and loving, why doesn't He bring to an end the world's suffering and the injustices that we see all around us?

Although these questions are easy to ask, they are difficult for the Christian to answer. Let me try to answer them, by first posing another question—Who is responsible for the evil, the destruction and all the injustices that we see in our world? The Scriptures provide an answer. Scripture teaches us that God created this world and then placed humanity in the midst of it, to rule and have dominion over it. After God finished His final act of creation He looked down on the work that He had completed and He declared that it was *very good* (Genesis 1:31). This God of creation loved His creatures so much that He imparted to them the unique dignity of being free moral agents. As free moral agents they had the ability to choose between obedience and disobedience and between evil and good.

Since the beginning of time, however, God has borne the brunt of the blame for all the disasters we see around us. We have made

God responsible. We learned the lesson of shifting responsibility from ourselves to God, or to others, from our first parents. God placed Adam and Eve in the Garden of Eden and gave them the privilege of choice: "*The LORD God took the man and put him in the Garden of Eden to work it and take care of it. And the LORD God commanded the man, 'You are free to eat from any tree in the garden; but you must not eat from the tree of the knowledge of good and evil, for when you eat of it you will surely die'*" (Genesis 2:15-17). Adam and Eve chose to disobey and chaos, sin and death entered into our world. The fall of humanity is outlined in Genesis:

> *Then the man and his wife heard the sound of the LORD God as he was walking in the garden in the cool of the day, and they hid from the LORD God among the trees of the garden. But the LORD God called to the man, "Where are you?" He answered, "I heard you in the garden, and I was afraid because I was naked; so I hid." And he said, "Who told you that you were naked? Have you eaten from the tree that I commanded you not to eat from?" The man said, "The woman you put here with me—she gave me some fruit from the tree, and I ate it."* (Genesis 3:8-12)

When God came to Adam and Eve to hold them accountable for their actions, they responded as most human beings do, by blaming others. Eve, who fed Adam from the tree, blamed the Serpent who beguiled her. And Adam? He blamed God—"the woman *you* put here with me." Since that time, humanity has been blaming one another and God for the evil that goes on in our world. Adam disobeyed God and tried to cover over his sin, and then he hid from God. But why did he hide? This was the same God who allowed Adam to name the animals and gave him complete dominion over the earth. The God who made a help-mate suitable for Adam and who had walked with Adam in the Garden in the cool of the day. So why was Adam hiding? Adam knew that he had broken fellowship and his covenant agreement with God. He knew he was in the wrong and that the punishment God had promised would follow. The punishment was death. Physical death did not follow immediately, and instead there was a two-fold spiritual death. That's why Adam was hiding. The mystical spiritual union between God and Adam had been broken. So also had the mystical spiritual union between Adam and Eve. Sin had entered the world and shattered the relationship between God and humanity and between men and women. What did it feel like to Adam? It felt as though he had lost everything. This is obvious from the way he addressed God and tried to shift the blame. Adam attempted to shift the responsibility for the fall to God. This example of blaming God for misfortune, sin and tragedy has been the pattern of humanity from the time of Adam. God makes an easy scapegoat, as He never defends Himself against the charges we levy against Him.

The Book of Job in the Old Testament is one of my favourite books, and a good one to study when we wrestle with the problem of why bad things happen to good people or why is there so much evil rampant in our world? Job was an excellent, God-fearing man surrounded by much prosperity. Satan, confident that Job would curse God to His face if he had to undergo fiery trials, was permitted by God to rob Job of his wealth, his children, and his health. Even after Job was stripped of all these, he shunned evil. He did feel, however, that he had been unfairly victimized, persecuted, robbed of every sign of God's favour, and for thirty-seven chapters, he delivers a passionate outburst of agony and anger at God. Still, though, he will not curse God. In chapter 19, we hear his words that are such a contrast with his previous cries, words that were celebrated by Handel in *Messiah*: *"I know that my Redeemer lives, and that in the end he will stand upon the earth. And after my skin has been destroyed, yet in my flesh I will see God; I myself will see him with my own eyes—I, and not another. How my heart yearns within me!"* (Job 19:25-29). God's reply to Job in chapters 38 to 42 is the longest single speech attributed to God in the Scriptures. From those chapters we catch a glimpse of the Divine Sovereignty of God. What is most interesting is that God does not offer to Job an explanation for his suffering. From that we can conclude as human beings that we see only a very small part of God's unfolding plan for this world and our individual lives. The comfort of the message of the Book of Job is that God supremely treasures the righteousness of the godly sufferer, and we must trust in Him, as the God who does only what is right.

There are many people who are angry and bitter at God. God is blamed for all the tragedies in our world. Why is it God's fault that this planet is so polluted and disease runs rampant in our world? Why is it God's fault that one third of the world uses up two thirds of the world's resources? Why is it God's fault that one third of our world goes to bed hungry night after night? Why is it God's fault when weather systems are out of control because of pollution and damage to the ozone layer? Why is God blamed when people kill each other with a variety of weapons? I could go on and on…of all the lessons we have learned from Adam, the one we have learned best is to shift the blame. We shift the blame to God. We hold God accountable for the sins others commit against us. We hold God accountable when bad things happen to good people. We know from reading further in Genesis, that God did not discard humanity. I would assume, however, that to Adam, it felt as though He had. He felt he had lost God, but God didn't give up on Adam. When God came looking for Adam, Adam ran and hid. He didn't want to be in the presence of holiness. But God knew that He couldn't leave Adam to his own devices. Adam had to be punished, with Eve and the serpent. Even when God handed out punishment, however, He promised that redemption would come one day. That redemption would come through His Son Jesus Christ.

When God created humanity, He refused to make us like puppets on a string dancing to any tune He chooses to play. He gave us the gift of free choice. We see this gift of God in action with our first parents in the Garden of Eden. When Adam and Eve chose to disobey God, physical and spiritual death entered our world. For a fuller understanding of this freedom of choice, I turn to the words of Henri Blocher in his book, *Evil and the Cross*. Blocher focuses on the evil which we find in our world, and reminds us that God's solution to that evil is the cross of Christ. In describing this gift of free choice, Blocher quotes three authors, Francois Laplantine, C.S. Lewis, and Francis Schaeffer.

> Laplantine writes: 'God does not create robots, puppets, or marionettes, but free human beings, free even to resist him, to say No to him, and to hang him on a cross. And that is what happened. Because the God of Jesus Christ is not a despot, an absolute monarch, a sovereign with limitless powers. The God of our Lord Jesus Christ withdraws from his creation, and forgoes the immediate completion of mankind and the world in order to allow human freedom to unfurl and create history. This incomplete state of the world is the cause of evil.' (Francois Laplantine in *Le Philosophe et la violence*)

> C.S. Lewis gives a vivid yet delicate portrayal of the sheer delight experienced by Paradisal man in his filial self-surrender to his Creator. But even in that state Lewis finds the possibility of sin: 'The mere existence of a self—the mere fact that we call it 'me'—includes, from the first, the danger of self-idolatry.' He calls this 'the weak spot' in the very nature of creation, the risk which God apparently thinks worth taking. (C.S. Lewis in *The Problem of Pain*)

> Francis Schaeffer, whose popular presentation of an apologetic for the latter half of the twentieth century has left its mark on a whole generation of young American Christians, presents as the solution to the problem of evil the argument that God 'created man as a non-determined person'. He is a being 'who could choose to obey the commandment of God and love Him, or revolt against Him.' (Francis Schaeffer, *The God Who Is There*)[17]

We need to understand that God is against evil and He recognizes that evil's existence is often a stumbling block to the belief in the God of Love. Scripture is very clear, however, that evil is the result of the abuse of the free will that God has granted to His creation, both angelic and human. Jesus combated many manifestations of evil, but God's answer to humanity's choice of evil is the Cross of Redemption.

The Scriptures place responsibility for sin, which opened up the floodgates of evil, at the feet of humanity. Paul said in his letter to the Romans that when sin entered our world through Adam's failure, all humanity was implicated. God did not, however, leave us in our lostness and destruction. He sent His Son into the world. This view of creation and sin is contrary to the culture in which we live. Many believe that nature created us and given enough time, we have the ability within ourselves to change the world in which we live. We have proven again and again, however, that humanity does not have the ability to change the hearts of human beings, where the change must first take place. The moral change that takes place through the Gospel is evidence of the victory over all evil powers and sin. (See Chapter 4, The Cross of Redemption)

The Good News of the Scripture is that God has not left us to our own devices. He has promised redemption and that redemption comes through His Son Jesus Christ. By being fully human Jesus knows and understands the suffering and injustices faced by many in our world.

I had the privilege recently of praying with a man who was dying. He asked me, "Why does the Lord permit such terrible things to happen in our world?" The only response that I could give was, "We as a society are reaping what we have sown. We have sown violence, destruction, hatred, and outright rebellion. The innocent have been caught in the fruit of our labours. Those labours have brought us destruction, increased violence and death. We want to blame God, but we are the ones who have sown the seeds. Be assured, though, God is not far from the suffering that runs rampant in our world."

The 1986 Nobel Peace Prize holder, Eli Wiesel, taken as a teenager to the Auschwitz and Buchenwald concentration camps, recorded his memoirs of that experience in his book, *Night.* He witnessed evil at its most shocking and absolute, and records being forced to watch the cruel hanging of a young boy.

> For more than half an hour he stayed there, struggling between life and death, dying in slow agony under our eyes. And we had to look him full in the face. He was still alive when I passed in front of him. His tongue was still red, his eyes were not yet glazed. Behind me, I heard the same man asking: 'Where is God now?' And I heard a voice within me answer him: 'Where is He? Here He is—He is hanging here on this gallows…'[18]

You may ask, "Where is Jesus when evil runs rampant in our world?" Let me assure you that in spite of what takes place, evil will not have the final word. I would also suggest, if you are searching for God in the midst of tragedies and terror, you would find Jesus present in those events. Jesus wanders through the school halls where the innocent have been slain. Jesus walks the streets of cities like New York, embracing those who are experiencing devastating pain. Jesus was not a stranger to refugee and concentration camps—He was there weeping with those who wept, and granting courage to those who were in despair. In his book, *The Cross of Christ*, John Stott includes the playlet entitled, *The Long Silence.* It seems appropriate to conclude this section on the Cross of Rejection, by sharing that playlet.

> At the end of time, billions of people were scattered on a great plain before God's throne. Most shrank back from the brilliant light before them. But some groups near the front talked heatedly—not with cringing shame, but with belligerence.
>
> 'Can God judge us? How can he know about suffering?' snapped a pert young brunette. She ripped open a sleeve to

reveal a tattooed number from a Nazi concentration camp. 'We endured terror... beatings... torture... death!'

In another group a Negro boy lowered his collar. 'What about this?' he demanded, showing an ugly rope burn. 'Lynched...for no crime but being black!'

In another crowd, a pregnant schoolgirl with sullen eyes, 'Why should I suffer' she murmured, 'It wasn't my fault.'

Far out across the plain there were hundreds of such groups. Each had a complaint against God for the evil and suffering he permitted in his world. How lucky God was to live in heaven where all was sweetness and light, where there was no weeping or fear, no hunger or hatred. What did God know of all that man had been forced to endure in this world? For God leads a pretty sheltered life, they said.

So each of these groups sent forth their leader, chosen because he had suffered the most. A Jew, a Negro, a person from Hiroshima, a horribly deformed arthritic, a thalidomide child. In the center of the plain they consulted with each other. At last they were ready to present their case. It was rather clever.

Before God could be qualified to be their judge, he must endure what they had endured. Their decision was that God should be sentenced to live on earth—as a man!

'Let him be born a Jew. Let the legitimacy of his birth be doubted. Give him a work so difficult that even his family will think him out of his mind when he tries to do it. Let him be betrayed by his closest friends. Let him face false charges, be tried by a prejudiced jury and convicted by a cowardly judge. Let him be tortured.

'At the last, let him see what it means to be terribly alone. Then let him die. Let him die so that there can be no doubt that he died. Let there be a great host of witnesses to verify it.'

As each leader announced his portion of the sentence, loud murmurs of approval went up from the throng of people assembled.

And when the last had finished pronouncing sentence, there

was a long silence. No one uttered another word. No one moved. For suddenly all knew that God had already served his sentence.[19]

CONSEQUENCES OF REJECTING JESUS

If we reject God's plan of salvation, we will die in our sins. Even in this scientific and technical age, most people living in the Western world acknowledge the cross of Jesus in some vague way. They feel very uncomfortable, however, when you talk about Jesus dying for them, or having shed His blood for the sins of the world. Some, like Gestas, would accept the benefits a Saviour King could grant, but not Jesus himself. One writer expressed it this way:

> The appeal of this malefactor was on a level with an effort to break free from prison. Just as a criminal might try to break out from prison, so this man in his last hour wanted to break away from his desperate plight. There seemed no thought in his mind of being rightly related to God, or of repenting of his sin and changing his way of life. His concern was an extension of his earthly life, maybe in order to go on living just as he had done before.[20]

Those who are in prison have a personal and palpable desire for liberation. They would like to be set free. Yet those who are not confined by bars and prison walls seem incapable of realizing their need for a personal Saviour. Many do not realize how imprisoned by sin they are. The Scriptures are very clear that God desires to rescue us and set us free from our self-imposed prisons. But He doesn't set us free so that we may continue to live our lives fulfilling the desires of the flesh and walking according to the ways of the world. In Romans, Paul put it like this,

> *Therefore, I urge you, brothers, in view of God's mercy, to offer your bodies as living sacrifices, holy and pleasing to God—this is your spiritual act of worship. Do not conform any longer to the pattern of*

this world, but be transformed by the renewing of your mind. Then you will be able to test and approve what God's will is—his good, pleasing and perfect will. (Romans 12:1-2)

God's desire for His children is that they live lives that are honouring to Him. When we accept Jesus, we are invited to leave behind our lives of sin and learn to walk in holiness and righteousness.

John the Apostle tells us two stories of Jesus' healing that are related to sin. The story of the man who had been crippled for thirty-eight years is told in the fifth chapter of John's Gospel. Jesus sets him free from this infirmity and then says to him: *"See, you are well again. Stop sinning or something worse may happen to you"* (John 5:14). The second story is well known. Through deceit and a desire to trap Jesus, the teachers of the law and the Pharisees brought a woman caught in the act of adultery before Jesus for judgment. Much to the disappointment of the gathered crowd, Jesus invited those who were without sin to cast the first stone. One by one, the members of the crowd left and Jesus and the woman were left alone. Jesus then asked her if any one condemned her. She responded, *"No one, sir,"* she said. *"Then neither do I condemn you,"* Jesus declared. *"Go now and leave your life of sin"* (John 8:11). In both these cases, Jesus did not condone the actions of the sinners, but invited them to leave behind their lives of sin.

We are invited to pursue a life of holiness, righteousness and obedience. That does not mean that we will not continue to wrestle with the sins of the world, the flesh and the devil. What it does mean is that we must not allow sin to be our master. In fact we are called to master sin. The first recorded murder in history took place when Cain murdered his brother Abel. Prior to the murder, God warned Cain, *"If you do what is right, will you not be accepted? But if you do not do what is right, sin is crouching at your door; it desires to have you, but you must master it"* (Genesis 4:7). In the seventh chapter of Romans, Paul tells us of his struggles with sin, and that he could not free himself from sin in his own strength. He acknowledged that he was a slave to sin and at the close of the chapter he said, *"What a wretched man I am! Who will rescue me from this body of death?"* Paul answered his own question by responding, *"Thanks be to God—through Jesus Christ our Lord!"* (Romans 7:25). It is only through Jesus that our sins are abolished and we are set free. When we are set free, we begin to walk in the grace of God and over time, we experience more and more freedom. In his Epistle, John wrote, *"No one who is born of God will continue to sin, because God's seed remains in him; he cannot go on sinning, because he has been born of God"* (1 John 3:9). The greatest difficulty for some people is not giving up sin, but acknowledging that one is a sinner.

Gestas never took responsibility for his sins. The word *sin* is not a very popular word in this day and age and I suspect it wasn't two thousand years ago. (For an explanation of sin, see the chapter on the Cross of Redemption.) There is an innate stubbornness within the heart and it refuses to acknowledge that one is a sinner. We are very satisfied with self-centered spirituality. If we do acknowledge God at all—it is normally a small God that we have formed in our own image. At the very centre of our spirituality is "self" and we like to think that we are Lord and Master of our own domain. We carry within ourselves an infinite capacity for self-deception. If we do believe in God, we do our very best to keep God on the margins of our lives awaiting our beck and call. The Scriptures insist, however, that God is sovereign, and that we all have to deal with Him as He reveals Himself, not as we imagine Him to be. Sadly, there are those of us who have become very much like the righteous ones of Jesus' day. We see that others may need to repent, but we never, as Jesus says, "take the planks out of our own eyes." We never see any need for our own repentance (Luke 6:42). On the other hand, there are those who no longer see a need for God in their lives, and if there is no need of God, they certainly will not have much use for salvation. At least, not for salvation that is offered from a cross. But if we reject the salvation of the cross, then like Gestas, we reject any possibility of living in eternity with God. In addition, we reject the gift of forgiveness that God freely wants to grant to each of us. Gestas may not have seen himself as a sinner. His conscience may have been seared or maybe he had no concept of sin. I find it easy to relate to Gestas for I lived a good part of my life without any real concept of God or of sin.

I had no real understanding of what personal sin was, and how offensive it was to God. I had no difficulty with the idea of corporate sin, but I saw myself as someone who was as righteous as the next person. In the last chapter of this book, I will tell you of the night of May 30, 1979, when God turned my life upside down and transformed me—the night I embraced the Cross of Redemption. It was such a life-changing encounter that I have never forgotten the date. I would like to tell you here, however, of a lesson God taught me several months after that first encounter that I have also never forgotten. I was member of the Canadian Forces stationed in Ottawa. As part of my duties, I traveled to various military bases teaching management principles. On this occasion, I was sent to the French language recruit-training base at St. Jean, Quebec. When I arrived at the base, I grabbed my suitcase and briefcase off the back seat of my car, and walked towards the main headquarters. In addition to all that I was carrying, I had my car keys in my hand. As I walked across the parking lot, the keys fell from my hand and dropped through the lid of a storm-sewer. I was completely lost without those keys. I went in to see the duty officer and discovered we had a major communication problem. I spoke broken French and he broken English. I managed to convey to him that I had dropped my keys in the sewer and he said he would get in touch with maintenance people who would see what they could do for me. In the meantime, I went out and stood on that sewer grate and began to pray. Without those keys, I couldn't get into my suitcase or my briefcase. Nor could I leave the base.

I stood on top of that sewer for an hour and a half. It was starting to get dark and I was beginning to panic. Off in the distance, I saw someone walking towards me with a long pole in his hand. As he got closer I could see that he was a maintenance man dressed in coveralls with rubber boots on his feet. I breathed a sigh of relief that the salvation of my keys seemed close at hand. When he got to the storm sewer, he plied up the grate with the pole he carried. He stuck the pole in the sewer and said to me, "It's not very deep." I responded, "Thank God." He then turned to me and said, "Those your keys?" and I said, "Yes." "Go get them," he said. I was standing over this sewer in my best dress uniform. My shoes were spit polished and he wanted me to climb into the sewer. He had the boots and coveralls and he was dressed for the task at hand. But he told me very clearly that he was a civilian maintenance worker and he had no intention of crawling down into a dirty sewer to rescue my keys. So the choice was up to me—did I want my keys or not? I took off my coat, rolled up my shirtsleeves, took off my shoes and socks and crawled down into that storm sewer.

Storm sewers are not very big and there is not a lot of space to turn around. I tried feeling for my keys with my toes, but located nothing. I was fortunate in that I wasn't a big man, and so I managed to get down on my hands and knees and feel around in the garbage that had accumulated in the sewer. I finally came up with my keys. By this time, I was absolutely filthy, but so delighted that I had found my keys. I went to my room and stepped into the shower, uniform and all. I also gave my keys the shower of their life. When I had finished, I sat down and asked God, "What are You trying to teach me?" I don't normally ask such questions, but I was so overwhelmed by the circumstances that I felt there had to be a reason for my keys falling into that sewer. That evening, God impressed upon my heart this lesson that I have never forgotten. He said to me, "Ron, I want you never to forget that I reached down into the filth, dirt and garbage of your life and pulled you up. I have given you the keys to the kingdom of Heaven. Go and tell others of the liberty and freedom that is to be found in My Son."

Until that night, I had never seen myself as a grievous sinner. I had never realized the filth and dirt that had accumulated in my life. I did not realize how offensive my sins were to God. I, like Gestas, did not know how far I had wandered from God. We know Gestas as a criminal who died next to Jesus, but he wasn't always a criminal. Through a series of choices he became a criminal. Although we inherit our sinful nature from Adam, we also make a series of choices, which distance us from God. When we commit a sin, it alerts our conscience, but after a time our conscience becomes seared and our heart grows cold. We no longer recognize that we are building a prison for ourselves. Jesus came to set us free from those prisons and if we reject His Father's plan of salvation, we will die in those sins.

Rejection of God's plan of salvation leaves us with an unhealthy and burdensome fear of judgment. Some may find the word *judgment* offensive, but judgment means that God holds His creation accountable and responsible for the choices it makes. John Stott writes,

> Our responsibility before God is an inalienable aspect of our human dignity…nobody will be sentenced without a trial. All people, great and small, irrespective of their social class, will stand before God's throne, not crushed or browbeaten, but given this final token of respect for human responsibility, as each gives an account of what he or she has done.[21]

Dismas said to Gestas, *"We are punished justly, for we are getting what our deeds deserve. But this man has done nothing wrong"* (Luke 23:41). Dismas readily admitted that the two of them were being punished justly for crimes they had committed. They had been found guilty and sentenced to death. The Roman Court held them responsible and accountable for their actions, and in less than six hours they would stand before the God of Justice for a similar type of judgment. In their case there is no question of guilt or innocence nor is there any suggestion that their punishment by crucifixion was a miscarriage of justice. We may think their sentence was reprehensible but under Roman law, the punishment for robbery with violence was crucifixion.

Although Dismas recognized that he would be judged for his actions, in this day and age the teaching of the Scriptures regarding judgment is in conflict with how the vast majority of people think. Why is it that most people today reject the idea that we will have to give an account of our lives when we die? The *New Bible Dictionary* succinctly defines the attitude of many in this generation.

> Our loss of conviction concerning an after-life, combined with the erosion of the notion of moral responsibility on the basis of popular understanding of psychological and psycho-analytical theories, has contributed to the moral indifference and pragmatism of our times. Moral issues, in so far as they matter at all, relate only to the present moment and to considerations of personal happiness. The thought that they might relate to some transcendent divine dimension, or that all people will one day be inescapably summoned to accept responsibility for those very moral decisions in the all-seeing presence of their Creator, is anathema.[22]

Scripture, however, says that judgment is inevitable and awaits us all. So let us have the courage to look closely at what the Bible reveals about this judgment.

GOD'S JUST JUDGMENT

In the Old Testament, God is seen as the *Judge of all the earth*, or better still, as the *God of Justice*. In Genesis, God tells Abraham that the stench of sin taking place in the cities of Sodom and Gomorrah is so grievous, He has come to judge them. Abraham intercedes for these cities and wants to know if the *God of Justice* will judge the righteous in the same way as the wicked? God assures Abraham that he will not (Genesis 18:16-33). This shows us that the judgment of

God is neither impersonal nor indiscriminate. It shows us very clearly that God's judgment is always linked to His character of mercy, righteousness and truth. By sparing Lot and his family God showed that, on one hand, His judgment brings deliverance for those who are righteous, and, on the other, punishment for those who are wicked. As you read through the Old Testament, you will note that when God does bring judgment on nations, or even upon His chosen people, He is always consistent. That is His nature. Nine times throughout the Old Testament you will find these or similar words:

> *The LORD, the LORD, the compassionate and gracious God, slow to anger, abounding in love and faithfulness, maintaining love to thousands, and forgiving wickedness, rebellion and sin. Yet he does not leave the guilty unpunished; he punishes the children and their children for the sin of the fathers to the third and fourth generation.* (Exodus 34:6-7)

There are some who think that the God who is presented in the Old Testament, is different from the God and Father that our Lord Jesus Christ came to reveal. Some think that between the last book of the Old Testament and the first book of the New Testament, God underwent a character change. In reading the Old Testament, some view God as a harsh, demanding, and overbearing judge. But that view of God is not consistent with Scripture. According to a true reading of the Scriptures, God has always been a loving God, who desires to embrace and love His people. God is always consistent in judging rightly and restoring those who wander from His paths. What has been inconsistent, both in life-style and attitude, and has caused great confusion, is the way in which others have presented the truths of the Scriptures.

Many in my generation grew up in a time when the emphasis of church teaching could only be described as "fire and brimstone." This type of teaching alienated many from God. How can you possibly love or be in a genuine relationship with someone you truly fear? In fact, you don't love those you fear; instead you grow to hate them as you await their inevitable punishment. When you live in fear of God's sudden judgment or punishment, your image of Him is truly distorted. As a consequence of those teachings, for more years than I care to admit, I absolutely despised God and everything He stood for. Yes, I know those are strong and disturbing words, but I confess I hated Him. That hatred burned like lava, deep into my soul. Instead of a heart of flesh and blood, there lived within me a heart of stone that was hard and unyielding. When your heart is stone, you become callous and unfeeling—and if you cannot feel, then you cannot be hurt. I know that my heart didn't become hard overnight. As a result of that erroneous teaching, combined with poor theology, seeds of hatred, bitterness and anger became deeply rooted within my heart during my early years. As I grew into adulthood, I began to distance myself from anything related to God. I am sad to confess, in fact, that God became my bitter enemy. If it weren't for His mercy and grace, I would probably have remained a God-hater. If I had been crucified on the left side of Jesus, I too would have railed against Him. Who then would have delivered me? Thank God, I can now say with the Apostle Paul—Jesus Christ is my Lord. As one who has come to know Jesus and understand the ways of God more fully, I am completely comfortable with the knowledge that the God of Justice is justifiably going to punish sin. God does not, however, desire the death of sinners.

I don't remember ever hearing as a child that our God of Justice was also a compassionate and loving Heavenly Father. I grew to view Him as an over-eager judge, gleefully waiting in anticipation of the punishment that He would eventually inflict. Since then, I have discovered that far too many in my generation have a similar distorted and harmful image of the God of mercy and love. He is not sitting around in expectation of the punishment to come; instead we learn from the Scriptures that it is God's desire for all people to come to Him in repentance. This message of repentance is spelled out very clearly in the New Testament.

The New Testament continues to stress that judgment belongs to God and is part of His essential activity. The message of God's impending judgment is revealed to us in different ways. When we begin reading the Gospels, we encounter Jesus' herald—John the Baptist. Those who came out to hear John were told that he, himself, was not the Messiah they were expecting, but only the forerunner to their Messiah. John warned the nation of Israel of the judgment to come, and his message was, *"Repent for the kingdom of Heaven is near"* (Matthew 3:2). He warned the people not to place their trust in the spirituality of their forbearers, but to produce their own fruit of repentance (Matthew 3:8). From this we learn that God holds each generation responsible for their response to God. (According to the Scriptures a generation is normally forty years.)

After Jesus was baptized and began His ministry, His message was consistent with John's, *"Repent, for the kingdom of heaven is near"* (Matthew 4:17). John and Jesus wanted to convey to the people that the very light of God had come into the world, and God was expecting a response to that messenger of light. I quoted John 3:16 earlier. In that passage we are told how much God loves this world, but following that message of love, comes a warning that we are invited to heed.

For God so loved the world that he gave his one and only Son, that whoever believes in him shall not perish but have eternal life. For God did not send his Son into the world to condemn the world, but to save the world through him. Whoever believes in him is not condemned, but whoever does not believe stands condemned already because he has not believed in the name of God's one and only Son. This is the verdict: Light has come into the world, but men loved darkness instead of light because their deeds were evil. Everyone who does evil hates the light, and will not come into the light for fear that his deeds will be exposed. But whoever lives by the truth comes

93

into the light, so that it may be seen plainly that what he has done has been done through God. (John 3:16-21)

So the first message in the New Testament regarding judgment is a message with an invitation of repentance attached. Our response to that invitation will disclose whether our profession to Jesus is the fruit of an honest and regenerated heart, or is only the mimicking of a hypocritical religion. That truth will be utterly exposed on a day that the New Testament calls *Judgment Day* or *the judgment to come.*

In many places in the New Testament we are told that there will be a future and final judgment that will accompany the return of Jesus to this earth (see Matthew 16:27; Romans 2:6; 2 Corinthians 5:10; Revelation 22:12). At that time, judgment will be based on a person's response to the revealed will of God. We will find as we read the New Testament that God's established and revealed will is that we acknowledge the Lordship of Jesus. We do this by turning from our wayward behaviour and embracing He whom God has sent. This genuine faith should express itself in a new and radical life-style, marked by a rejection of personal sin and made obvious by works of loving service for the glory of God. Paul put it this way: *"God will bring to light what is hidden in darkness and will expose the motives of people's hearts. At that time each will receive their praise from God"* (1 Corinthians 4:5b). When we read passages about the Day of Judgment, it is right to ask: "When will this take place?" The answer remains totally in the Father's care. This was one of the questions that the disciples asked Jesus. His response was, *"No one knows about that day or hour, not even the angels in heaven, nor the Son, but only the Father. Be on guard! Be alert! You do not know when that time will come"* (Mark 13:32-33). Although we do not know when that time will come, be assured that it **will** come. Peter warns us:

First of all, you must understand that in the last days scoffers will come, scoffing and following their own evil desires. They will say, "Where is this 'coming' he promised? Ever since our fathers died,

THE CROSS OF REJECTION

everything goes on as it has since the beginning of creation." (2 Peter 3:3-4)

That is the attitude of many people today. They don't believe that there will be a Day of Accounting. It is reasonable to ask: "Why does it seem that the Lord is slow in coming and this Day of Judgment has not yet come to pass?" Peter also supplies us with that answer:

> *But do not forget this one thing, dear friends: With the Lord a day is like a thousand years, and a thousand years are like a day. The Lord is not slow in keeping his promise, as some understand slowness. He is patient with you, not wanting anyone to perish, but everyone to come to repentance. But the day of the Lord will come like a thief. The heavens will disappear with a roar; the elements will be destroyed by fire, and the earth and everything in it will be laid bare.* (1 Peter 3:8-10)

God is patient with all of us, because He does not want anyone to perish. He wants all of us to come to repentance, and to have within our hearts a willingness to bow to the Lordship of Jesus. Yes, the day will come when every person in every generation will bow before Jesus. Not only will they bow, they will also confess the Lordship of Jesus, to the glory of God the Father (Philippians 2:10-11). How much better it will be for each of us if that is the true desire of our hearts.

We are also assured in the New Testament that all people will face judgment. The writer to the Hebrews says that a person is destined to die once, and after that to face judgment (Hebrews 9:27). Every aspect of our lives will come into account, including the secrets of the heart, which Jesus warned us would include every careless word. *"But I tell you that men will have to give account on the Day of Judgment for every careless word they have spoken. For by your words you will be acquitted, and by your words you will be condemned"* (Matthew 12:36-37). Even those who know and love God will be called upon to give an accounting of their lives. Jesus' disciples will be judged with respect to the stewardship of the talents, gifts, opportunities and responsibilities granted during the course of their lives. "The divine judgment of the people of God will be a Fatherly judgment. It will not be such as to place in peril the Christian's standing within the family of God; it will have all of a father's understanding and compassion; and yet it is not therefore to be lightly or carelessly regarded. This fatherly judgment will be exercised by Christ at his coming."[23]

My purpose in sharing this information about judgment is so that you may know that knowledge of future judgment is always a summons to present repentance. It is only those who are truly penitent who will be prepared for judgment when it finally comes. Luke tells us that Dismas was repentant and therefore, had no reason to fear future judgment. After he reached out to Jesus, he was immediately assured a place in God's paradise. There is no indication that Gestas repented and therefore he had every reason to fear the judgment that was to come when his life drew painfully to a close.

Another consequence of rejection is that we can die not only a physical death but a spiritual death as well. When Dismas cried out to Jesus, *"Remember me,"* Jesus responded to that cry by telling him that before the day was out, he would be with Jesus in Paradise. That was a dying Saviour's promise to a dying thief. We have no reason to believe that Jesus' promise was unfulfilled. But what happened to Gestas when he died? There are some frightening passages of Scripture that describe the final destiny of the godless and unrepentant. In Revelation, Jesus said to John:

> *"It is done. I am the Alpha and the Omega, the Beginning and the End. To him who is thirsty I will give to drink without cost from the spring of the water of life. He who overcomes will inherit all this, and I will be his God and he will be my son. But the cowardly, the unbelieving, the vile, the murderers, the sexually immoral, those who practice magic arts, the idolaters and all liars—their place will be in the fiery lake of burning sulphur. This is the second death."* (Revelation 21:6-8)

THE CROSS OF REJECTION

In my sixteen years as a pastor, I don't believe that I have ever preached on the final destiny of those who reject Jesus. I have often preached on the glories of heaven, but I have resisted expounding on this particular subject. One hesitates to write about such things, and rightly so, but they are part of the whole counsel of God. In writing on this matter here, I lean heavily upon a noted scholar and theologian, J.I. Packer, for his wisdom and insight into this difficult and yet challenging topic. He writes:

> The sentimental secularism of modern Western culture, with its exalted optimism about human nature, its shrunken idea of God, and its skepticism as to whether personal morality really matters—in other words, its decay of conscience—makes it hard for Christians to take the reality of hell seriously. The revelation of hell in Scripture assumes a depth of insight into divine holiness and human and demonic sinfulness that most of us do not have. However, the doctrine of hell appears in the New Testament as a Christian essential, and we are called to try to understand it as Jesus and his apostles did.[24]

In speaking about *Gehenna*, the Greek word we translate "hell," Jesus refers to it as a place of incineration (Matthew 5:22; 18:9). He also says it is the final home of those who have been consigned to eternal punishment (Matthew 25:41-46; Revelation 20:11-15). The New Testament tells us that hell is a place of fire, of darkness, of weeping and gnashing of teeth, of destruction and of torment (Jude 7, 13; Matthew 8:12, 13:42, 50; 2 Thessalonians 1:7-9; 2 Peter 3:7; Revelation 20:10).[25] All of these descriptions are, in many ways, far beyond our imagination. I don't believe that they are in the Scriptures to fill us with unbearable fear. Instead they are a warning and a call to us to come to a place of holiness, to a change of life-style and to repentance. The most frightening of the verses of Scripture listed above is one found in 2 Thessalonians. It reads: "*They will be punished with everlasting destruction and shut out from the presence of the Lord and from the majesty of his glory*" (2 Thessalonians 1:9). The thought of fire, deep darkness, and the gnashing of teeth is appalling enough, but to be shut out of God's presence for all eternity is horrifying. I cannot think of a worse fate. Scripture indicates that this separation and the punishment that goes with it, is unending. There is no second chance. I know that some have grown up with the doctrine of purgatory. Purgatory was to be the place of second chance, a place where one went after death to be purged of their sins. This doctrine came into being during the eighth century. According to the Anglican Articles of Religion however, the Canonical Books of both the Old and New Testament cannot prove this doctrine of purgatory.[26] If purgatory exists, then one could easily conclude that the sacrifice of Jesus for the sins of the world was not sufficient. That concept is repugnant and has no biblical warrant.

As I finish off this section on hell, I will return to the writings of J.I. Packer. Although the following is a long passage, it needs to be quoted in its entirety.

> Scripture sees hell as self-chosen; those in hell will realize that they sentenced themselves to it by loving darkness rather than light, choosing not to have their Creator as their Lord, preferring self-indulgent sin to self-denying righteousness, and (if they encountered the Gospel) rejecting Jesus rather than coming to him. General revelation confronts all mankind with this issue, and from this standpoint hell appears as God's gesture of respect for human choice. All receive what they actually chose, either to be with God forever, worshiping him, or without God forever, worshiping themselves. Those who are in hell will know not only that for their doings they deserve it but also that in their hearts they chose it. The purpose of the Bible teaching about hell is to make us appreciate, thankfully embrace, and rationally prefer the grace of Christ that saves us from it. It is really a mercy to mankind that God in Scripture is so explicit about hell. We cannot now say that we have not been warned.[27]

I want to leave you with this last thought about the consequences of rejecting Jesus. We have been given neither the right nor the responsibility to determine the final destiny of any person and that includes ourselves. Paul said,

> I care very little if I am judged by you or by any human court; indeed, I do not even judge myself. My conscience is clear, but that does not make me innocent. It is the Lord who judges me. Therefore judge nothing before the appointed time; wait till the Lord comes. He will bring to light what is hidden in darkness and will expose the motives of men's hearts. At that time each will receive his praise from God. (1 Corinthians 4:3-5)

The New Testament Scriptures say that the Father has entrusted all judgment to His Son Jesus Christ (John 5:22). He is the one to whom each one of us will have to give account. Jesus' judgment on each of us will be more than fair. We need to remember that Jesus laid down His life, not only for His friends, but also for those that despised and hated Him. He died for me and He died for Gestas. Although Gestas rejected the opportunity to turn to Jesus, let us be very clear that Jesus alone has been entrusted with the responsibility of determining one's punishment or one's reward. In the twenty-first chapter of John, we have the lovely story of the reinstatement of Simon Peter after his betrayal of the Lord. Simon Peter wanted to know what was going to happen to John, the beloved disciple. Jesus told Peter that he should not be concerned about John, and commanded Peter, *"Follow me."* Our time should not be spent in speculating about the lostness of others, or even the rewards of the faithful. Our time and energy should be spent in the pursuit of holiness and in genuine repentance for the sins for which we are responsible.

Gestas, hanging on the cross on Jesus' left, spent his time while dying cursing the One who had the power to take away the awful sting of death. Gestas was a dying sinner who was born in sin and died in sin. Regretfully, on the Cross of Rejection he died *full* of sin.

CHAPTER 4

THE CROSS OF REDEMPTION

Two other men, both criminals, were also led out with him to be executed. When they came to the place called the Skull, there they crucified him, along with the criminals—one on his right, the other on his left. Jesus said, "Father, forgive them, for they do not know what they are doing." And they divided up his clothes by casting lots. The people stood watching, and the rulers even sneered at him. They said, "He saved others; let him save himself if he is the Christ of God, the Chosen One." The soldiers also came up and mocked him. They offered him wine vinegar and said, "If you are the king of the Jews, save yourself." There was a written notice above him, which read: THIS IS THE KING OF THE JEWS. (Luke 23:32-38)

It is an historical fact that Jesus Christ of Nazareth was crucified. The writers of the four Gospels end their accounts by telling us of the final days of Jesus' life. According to their testimony those days were ones of great suffering. Although the Gospel writers do not go into the details of how Jesus' crucifixion was carried out, all four Gospels say, *"they crucified him."* The historical accounts of Jesus' crucifixion are not limited to the Holy Scriptures. Contemporary Christian, Jewish and Roman authors provide additional insight

100

concerning the first-century Jewish and Roman legal systems and the details of scourging and crucifixion.[1] Seneca, Livy, Plutarch and others refer to crucifixion practices in their works.[2] In addition, Jesus and His crucifixion is mentioned by the Roman historians Cornelius Tacitus, Pliny the Younger and Suetonius. It is also mentioned by the non-Roman historians Thallus and Phlegon; by the satirist Lucian of Samosata; by the Jewish Talmud and by the Jewish historian Flavius Josephus who called crucifixion "the most pitiable of deaths." [3,4]

As far as we know, crucifixion was not an invention of the Romans. Historians believe that it began first among the Persians.[5] Alexander the Great introduced the practice to Egypt and Carthage and the Romans appear to have learned of it from the Carthaginians.[6] The Romans took on the practice of crucifixion and perfected it as a form of torture and capital punishment that was designed to produce a slow death with maximum pain and suffering.[7]

On this third cross, which I have called the Cross of Redemption, hung a sign that identified the crucified man as the 'King of the Jews.' It is possible that Pilate meant this sign to be hung above Jesus' head in order to mock the Jewish leaders. It is also possible that as a further sign of his disdain for them, he had two criminals crucified at the same time as Jesus. These leaders had backed Pilate into a corner and the only public way that Pilate could strike back was through mockery. The "King" they had brought to Pilate for judgment was now hanging on a cross in the company of two "subjects" of the worst kind. The important thing is not what Pilate did, however, but what God did through Pilate. Although Pilate was not aware of it, he brought to fulfillment Old Testament prophecy that stated that the suffering servant would *be numbered with the transgressors* (Isaiah 53:12b).

We need to pay close attention to the sign above Jesus' head. It was common practice for the Romans to identify the crime for which they had been condemned on a plaque above the prisoner's head. John tells us:

Pilate had a notice prepared and fastened to the cross. It read: JESUS OF NAZARETH, THE KING OF THE JEWS. Many of the Jews read this sign, for the place where Jesus was crucified was near the city, and the sign was written in Aramaic, Latin and Greek. The chief priests of the Jews protested to Pilate, "Do not write 'The King of the Jews', but that this man claimed to be king of the Jews." Pilate answered, "What I have written, I have written." (John 19:19-22)

Every passer-by could read the signs, for everyone could read Aramaic (which is a form of the Hebrew language), Latin or Greek, the three great languages of the ancient world. In first-century Palestine, Latin was the language of government, and the language of the conqueror—Rome. Greek was the language of the older culture, the one which most people used day to day throughout the Roman Empire. It was also the one used and preferred by the cultural elite. Hebrew was the language of religion, the one used by Jews as they reached out to God. Ironically Pilate, by writing in all three major languages, was identifying Jesus' kingship over religion, culture and government, hence kingship over the whole world.[8]

In the last hours of His life, this King was subjected to tremendous verbal abuse as insults and jeers were hurled at His cross. I have shared with you the story of the criminal who mocked Jesus on the cross, but on that Good Friday there were three other groups of people on Calvary Hill. Onlookers were restricted from approaching any victim on a cross to strike them, but they struck Jesus again and again with the venom of their tongues. Jesus was crucified on a hill overlooking the main thoroughfare just outside the city of Jerusalem. Matthew's Gospel tells us that crowds of people walked by and hurled insults at Him, shaking their heads and saying, *"You who are going to destroy the temple and build it in three days, save yourself. Come down from the cross, if you are the Son of God!"* (Matthew 27:38-39). Many of these people may have been part of the same crowd that had welcomed

Jesus into Jerusalem a week before with the words, *"Hosanna to the Son of David"* (Matthew 21:9b).

Although many passed by hurling their insults, there were others at the site of the cross taunting Jesus. Among them were the Chief Priests, the Scribes and the Pharisees—Jesus' principal enemies. He had aroused their anger very early in His ministry. His attitude to the law and to the Sabbath in particular infuriated them, and almost from the very beginning of His ministry, they looked for an opportunity to kill Him. He was now dying upon the cross and, although it was the eve of the Passover, they could not bear to tear themselves away from Calvary. They were at the cross to gloat over their victory and to witness the death of Jesus. He had slipped through their hands on numerous occasions and on this day they wanted to make sure nothing went wrong.

> *In the same way the chief priests, the teachers of the law and the elders mocked him. "He saved others," they said, "but he can't save himself! He's the King of Israel! Let him come down now from the cross, and we will believe in him. He trusts in God. Let God rescue him now if he wants him, for he said, 'I am the Son of God.'"* (Matthew 27:41-43)

These leaders did not deny that Jesus had helped and saved many, but now He was powerless. His present helplessness made Him the object of their derision. These leaders were convinced that God had abandoned Jesus and they themselves were God's instruments in punishing this so called "Messiah." They would wait at the cross until He died and then they would go and eat the Passover meal with a clear conscience. With Jesus out of the way they could continue their spiritual domination over the people without interference.

The Gospel of Luke tells us that the soldiers also joined in the mockery of Jesus: *"The soldiers also came up and mocked him. They offered him wine vinegar and said, 'If you are the King of the Jews, save yourself'"* (Luke 23:36-37). These soldiers probably knew nothing about Jesus' teaching. In addition, they would have been surprised and probably quite shocked to find so many Jewish leaders at the crucifixion site. They took their cue from the crowd around them to mock Jesus as a King.

We may not be in agreement with the judgment given the two who were crucified with Jesus, but we can understand their fate. Their punishment was what the law demanded and permitted. But what about the man they called "the King of the Jews?" How did He get there? But more importantly, why was He there?

According to the Jewish system of justice, once Jesus had been tried and convicted of a capital crime, He could have been stoned to death and His body hung on a tree. Such an action by the Jewish authorities would have been in keeping with the laws laid down by Moses in the book of Deuteronomy, *"If a man guilty of a capital offence is put to death and his body is hung on a tree, you must not leave his body on the tree overnight. Be sure to bury him that same day, because anyone who is hung on a tree is under God's curse"* (Deuteronomy 21:22-23). In Jesus' time, the nation of Israel was under the rule of Rome. In order for the Jews to have someone sentenced to death, they needed special dispensation from the Roman Governor.

Under Roman law, Jesus Christ should not have been crucified. Crucifixion was reserved for slaves, foreigners, revolutionaries and the vilest of criminals. Jesus did not fit into any of these categories. What were the circumstances then, that led up to this event?

To answer those questions, we need to examine the last night of Jesus' life as recorded in the Scriptures. Although the four Gospel narratives are similar in content, they differ in their finer details. By putting the four Gospels together, however, we have a clear picture of Jesus' last hours before His crucifixion. Let us look at the significant events that took place just before the crucifixion.

EVENTS OF THE NIGHT BEFORE

The biblical record tells us that in the hours before the crucifixion, Jesus had gathered with His disciples in Jerusalem to share in the Passover meal—the one that has become known as The Last Supper. Two highly significant events took place during this supper.

NEW COVENANT

Luke tells us that in the last week of Jesus' life, He spent the days teaching in the temple, and in the evenings went out to the hill called the Mount of Olives. Then as the feast of the Passover approached,

> *Jesus sent Peter and John, saying, "Go and make preparations for us to eat the Passover." "Where do you want us to prepare for it?" they asked. He replied, "As you enter the city, a man carrying a jar of water will meet you. Follow him to the house that he enters, and say to the owner of the house, 'The Teacher asks: Where is the guest room, where I may eat the Passover with my disciples?' He will show you a large upper room, all furnished. Make preparations there."* (Luke 22:8-12)

Memorial services or funerals are normally held after a person has died. Although the disciples may not have realized what was happening, a memorial service actually took place that night. For it is here that Jesus gave His last command to His disciples. That command was to carry on the Last Supper. He specifically said to them, *"do this in remembrance of me"* (Luke 22:19). What were they to do? They were to repeat His actions and His words: *"And he took bread, gave thanks and broke it, and gave it to them, saying; 'This is my body given for you; do this in remembrance of me.' In the same way, after the supper he took the cup, saying, 'This cup is the new covenant in my blood, which is poured out for you'"* (Luke 22:19-20). The bread symbolized His body—a body that soon would be broken for each of them in death. The wine symbolized His blood—blood that would shortly be *"poured out"* or as Matthew wrote, *"shed for the forgiveness of sins"* (Matthew 26:28). John Stott writes in *The Cross of Christ,*

> The evidence is plain and irrefutable. The Lord's Supper which was instituted by Jesus, and which is the only regular commemorative act authorized by him, dramatizes neither his birth, nor his life, neither his words (teachings) nor his works, but only his death. Nothing could indicate more clearly the central significance, which Jesus attached to his death. It was by his death that he wished above all else to be remembered. There is then, it is safe to say, no Christianity without the cross. If the cross is not central to our religion, ours is not the religion of Jesus.[9]

The Apostle Paul also picks up on this theme in his Epistle to the troubled Church of Corinth. Abuse of this memorial service was happening, and so Paul exhorted them with these words:

> *I speak to sensible people; judge for yourselves what I say. Is not the cup of thanksgiving for which we give thanks a participation in the blood of Christ? And is not the bread that we break a participation in the body of Christ? Because there is one loaf, we, who are many, are one body, for we all partake of the one loaf.* (1 Corinthians 10: 15-17)

In the very next chapter Paul tells this Church, and in a sense all churches, that we are to continue in the practice of breaking bread and drinking wine until the Lord returns:

> *In the same way, after supper he took the cup, saying, "This cup is the new covenant in my blood; do this, whenever you drink it, in remembrance of me." For whenever you eat this bread and drink this cup, you proclaim the Lord's death until he comes.* (1 Corinthians 11:25-26)

Something else took place in the Upper Room during their supper that evening. Luke records these words: *"In the same way, after the supper he took the cup, saying, 'This cup is the new covenant in my blood, which is poured out for you'"* (Luke 22:20). Jesus meant that on this very night, God had taken the initiative in establishing a new covenant, a covenant that would be established in Jesus' name, which included the removal of sins. Centuries earlier, God had entered into a covenant with His chosen people, the Israelites. When that covenant was ratified with the blood of sacrifice, Moses was given specific instructions and words to say to the Israelites: *"Moses then took the blood, sprinkled it on the people and said: 'This is the blood of the covenant that the Lord has made with you in accordance with these words'"* (Exodus 24:8). This covenant, however, was a limited covenant. It was restricted to the nation of Israel and required obedience to the laws laid down by Moses as he had received them from God. The people found it impossible though, to be true to the covenant. They turned their back on God and abandoned His ways and His commandments again and again, but God had a plan of rescue, not only for the nation of Israel, but eventually for all the nations of the world.

This new covenant would not be written on tablets of stone, but on the hearts of people. This new covenant would not be contingent on human obedience, but would be a work of God's Spirit. In the seventh century B.C. the word of the Lord came to the Prophet Jeremiah:

> *"The time is coming," declares the LORD, "when I will make a new covenant with the house of Israel and with the house of Judah. It will not be like the covenant I made with their forefathers when I took them by the hand to lead them out of Egypt, because they broke my covenant, though I was a husband to them," declares the LORD. "This is the covenant I will make with the house of Israel after that time," declares the LORD. "I will put my law in their minds and write it on their hearts. I will be their God, and they will be my people. No longer will a man teach his neighbour, or a man his brother, saying, 'Know the LORD,' because they will all know me, from the least of them to the greatest," declares the LORD.*

"For I will forgive their wickedness and will remember their sins no more." (Jeremiah 31:31-40)

On this last night of Jesus' life, He made the promise that the time was at hand for the new covenant to be established. Like the covenants of old, it too would be ratified with blood. The blood of the spotless Lamb of God!

BETRAYAL BY JUDAS

The other significant event to take place during the supper gathering was Jesus' betrayal by His close friend and chosen disciple, Judas. During this meal Jesus told his disciples that one of them would betray him. *"I tell you the truth, one of you is going to betray me"* (John 13:21). This is how John records that event:

> *His disciples stared at one another, at a loss to know which of them he meant. One of them, the disciple whom Jesus loved, was reclining next to him. Simon Peter motioned to this disciple and said, "Ask him which one he means." Leaning back against Jesus, he asked him, "Lord, who is it?" Jesus answered, "It is the one to whom I will give this piece of bread when I have dipped it in the dish." Then, dipping the piece of bread, he gave it to Judas Iscariot, son of Simon. As soon as Judas took the bread, Satan entered into him. "What you are about to do, do quickly," Jesus told him, but no one at the meal understood why Jesus said this to him. Since Judas had charge of the money, some thought Jesus was telling him to buy something for the Feast, or to give something to the poor. As soon as Judas had taken the bread, he went out. And it was night.* (John 13:22-31)

Judas is listed in the synoptic Gospels as one of the twelve Jesus called *"to be with him"* (Mark 3:14). In the list of the apostles, Judas' name always appeared last and was accompanied by a description, which branded him with a notorious stigma. In the apostolic band, Judas was the treasurer and in chapter 12 of John's Gospel he was described as a thief who pilfered the money, which was entrusted to him. He was the one who spoke against Mary, the sister of Lazarus, who anointed Jesus' feet with pure nard, an expensive anointing oil, shortly before His death. John's intention was to stress the greed of Judas. The price of the oil blocked Judas' capacity to see the beauty of the deed that Jesus praised. In fact, in Matthew's Gospel, Jesus said, *"When she poured this perfume on my body, she did it to prepare me for burial. I tell you the truth, wherever this Gospel is preached throughout the world, what she has done will also be told, in memory of her"* (Matthew 21:12-13). The suggestion is that Judas' intention was to sell the perfume and use the money, not to help the poor, but to line his own pockets. It was after the incident of Mary's anointing of Jesus, that Judas approached the Chief Priests. He requested money in return for betraying Jesus and turning Him over to them:

> *Then one of the Twelve—the one called Judas Iscariot—went to the chief priests and asked, "What are you willing to give me if I hand him over to you?" So they counted out for him thirty silver coins. From then on Judas watched for an opportunity to hand him over.* (Matthew 26:14-16)

As we read the biblical record we can see that Jesus was not monstrously shocked that one of His own would betray Him. *"The Son of Man will go just as it is written about him. But woe to that man who betrays the Son of Man! It would be better for him if he had not been born"* (Matthew 26:24).

Two questions come to mind. First, why did Judas betray Jesus? It may have been because of his love of money or jealousy of the other disciples. It may have been an enthusiastic but misguided intention to force Jesus' hand and make Him declare himself publicly as the Messiah and then lead an open rebellion against Rome. Or, it could have been that Judas carried within his heart a bitter, vindictive spirit, which rose up when his worldly hopes were crushed. His disappointment turned to spite, and that spite turned to hate. These are some of the suggested motives for Judas' betrayal.

Secondly, why did Jesus select Judas as one of the twelve? We should not doubt the sincerity of the Lord's call upon Judas' life. Jesus, in selecting Judas, viewed him as a potential follower and disciple. Over the three years they journeyed together, I cannot imagine that Jesus treated Judas any differently than He treated the other disciples. Jesus would have considered him a friend. In hindsight, it is easy to see that Judas was never really Jesus' man. He fell from apostleship and as the biblical record shows, Judas never seemed to have a genuine relationship with the Lord Jesus. He remained *"the son of perdition"* (John 17:12, KJV) who was lost because he was never willing to be truly "found." According to the Gospels, the highest title Judas used for Jesus was "Rabbi" or "Teacher" but never "Lord." Judas lives in the pages of Scripture as a vivid warning to the uncommitted follower of Jesus who wants to be in Jesus' company, but does not share in the spirit of Christ. Judas left the Upper Room of his own choice, and was a doomed and damned man because he chose to betray Jesus. Make no mistake, Jesus loved and served Judas as much as He did the other apostles. The Apostle John indicates clearly that Judas was in the Upper Room the night that Christ washed the disciples' feet (John 13:5). Jesus did this to show them how much He truly loved them and wanted to serve them.

One of the fallacies regarding Judas, which is evident in many artists' paintings, is that he is portrayed as a sly, conniving fellow. The truth of the matter is that he was one of the selected twelve. He was one of the chosen. Although he was not part of the intimate inner circle, which included Peter, James and John, he was always one of the twelve. There is little doubt that initially, at least, Judas was a popular and trusted member of the apostles' group, since they appointed him treasurer. They must have done so because they believed that he would do the right thing with the funds entrusted to his care. Judas' betrayal of Jesus more than likely wounded Jesus deeply, but it must have devastated the apostles.

Sometimes there is no way to comprehend betrayal. In February 2001, Robert Phillip Hanssen, a twenty-five year veteran of the FBI, was arrested and accused of spying and selling the United States' most classified information to the Soviet Union over a period of fifteen years. According to law sources, Robert Hanssen was the most prolific and damaging spy in U.S. history. He stole secrets not only from the FBI, but also from the CIA, the White House, the Pentagon, and the National Security Agency. He received over $1.4 million in cash and diamonds in return for his spying efforts. Robert Hanssen was a well-respected member of an honourable organization. He was a family man, very involved in his community and local church. His partners, with whom he fought crime and espionage for twenty-five years, were astounded at his arrest. They wanted to know why would he betray his co-workers? Why would he betray his wife and children? Why would he betray the country he had sworn to protect? Why would he betray his church and beliefs? Finally, why would he betray his God? In May of 2002, Robert Hanssen received a sentence of life in prison with no chance of parole.[10] All the questions remain unanswered. No one knows why Robert Hanssen chose to betray those closest to him. Similarly, no one truly knows what was going on in the heart of Judas when he decided to betray Jesus for thirty pieces of silver. If there is anything that can be learned from Judas' betrayal, it is this. If someone betrays you, someone you love or consider a close friend, then know that Jesus understands what it means and how it feels, to be deceived by someone you love and trust. Someone close enough that they would dare to kiss you as they betray you: *"Even my close friend, whom I trusted, he who shared my bread, has lifted up his heel against me"* (Psalm 41:9).

According to Matthew's Gospel, after Jesus had been arrested, Judas was filled with remorse and returned the thirty pieces of silver to the Chief Priests and Elders, and then he went out and hanged himself. Remorse is not repentance. Remorse and regret come about because one has been caught. The returned money was used to buy a potter's field as a burial place for foreigners, thus, says Matthew, fulfilling what was spoken of by Jeremiah the Prophet:

> *They took the thirty silver coins, the price set on him by the people of Israel, and they used them to buy the potter's field as the Lord commanded me.* (Matthew 27:9-10)

TRIAL BEFORE THE SANHEDRIN

After Judas' betrayal of Him in the Garden of Gethsemane, Jesus was immediately brought to trial. Certain Jewish laws were supposed to be observed when an accused came to trial before the Chief Priest and the Sanhedrin. On the night of Jesus' betrayal, most of these laws were broken.

Trials could occur only in the regular meeting places of the Sanhedrin, not in the palace of the High Priest. According to John's testimony, Jesus was brought first to Annas, the father-in-law of Caiaphas, the high priest. Annas questioned Jesus about His disciples and about His teaching. Jesus' response to Annas was,

> *"I have spoken openly to the world. I have always taught in syna-gogues or at the temple, where all the Jews come together. I have said nothing in secret. Why question me? Ask those who heard me. Surely they know what I said."* (John 18:19-21)

For that response, Jesus was struck across the face by one of Annas' officials.

Trials were never to occur on the eve of the Sabbath or Feast Days or at night. At the time of Jesus' arrest, the Hebrews were celebrating the Feast of Unleavened Bread. This was a week-long celebration commemorating the Israelites' exodus from Egypt. *"Celebrate the Feast of Unleavened Bread; for seven days eat bread made without yeast, as I commanded you"* (Exodus 23:15).

When the accused was tried, a sentence of 'guilty' could only be pronounced on the day following the trial.

In addition, the Sanhedrin did not have the authority to instigate charges. They could only investigate charges brought before them.

Jesus was not permitted any kind of defence. According to the Jewish law, an exhaustive search into the facts presented by the witnesses should have taken place.[11]

When anyone was charged with crimes against God or the nation of Israel, they could not be convicted on the testimony of witnesses who were not in agreement. Matthew tells us that many false witnesses came forward, but evidence could not be found to convict Jesus, let alone establish that He should be put to death: "*On the testimony of two or three witnesses a man shall be put to death, but no one shall be put to death on the testimony of only one witness. The hands of the witnesses must be the first in putting him to death, and then the hands of all people*" (Deuteronomy 17:6-7).

In the trial itself, Jesus was charged with blasphemy because of allegations by witnesses that Jesus said He would destroy the temple of God and rebuild it in three days. Along with the charge of blasphemy was the charge that He "declared himself to be the *Son of God.*" As Jesus stood before the High Priest, He was silent. He did not respond to the charges against Him. So the High Priest asked him directly, "*Are you the Christ, the Son of the Blessed One?' 'I AM,' said Jesus*" (Mark 14:61b-62). By responding the way he did, Jesus used a phrase that was reserved for God. This phrase occurred in the Jewish Scriptures in several places. The very first occurrence was recorded in Exodus when Moses said to God in front of the burning bush,

> "*Suppose I go to the Israelites and say to them, 'The God of your fathers has sent me to you,' and they ask me, 'What is his name?' Then what shall I tell them?" God said to Moses, "I AM WHO I AM. This is what you are to say to the Israelites: 'I AM has sent me to you.'*" (Exodus 3:13-14)

Jesus' response to Caiaphas would have horrified the court. He then said to Caiaphas, "*And you will see the Son of Man sitting at the right hand of the Mighty One and coming on the clouds of heaven"* (Mark 14:62). This second proclamation was a direct reference to and description of the promised Messiah from the prophet Daniel (Daniel 7:13). With those words, Caiaphas determined that Jesus was guilty of blasphemy. Along with the Sanhedrin who had gathered for the trial, he decided that Jesus should be put to death. After this pronouncement, the crowd turned on Jesus: *"Then some began to spit at him; they blindfolded him, struck him with their fists, and said 'Prophesy!' And the guards took him and beat him"* (Mark 14:65).

After this mockery of a trial, Jesus was brought to Pilate, the Roman Governor, because neither the High Priest nor the Sanhedrin wished to soil their hands with His blood. Furthermore, for the Sanhedrin to put someone to death, they needed Rome's approval. On the other hand, if Pilate gave them that authority, the priests recognized that the crowds who had followed Jesus into Jerusalem the week before could turn on them. It was more prudent to turn Jesus over to Pilate and thus blame Rome for His death. When they brought Jesus to Pilate, however, the charges against Jesus had changed. No longer was He charged with heresy or blasphemy, but with sedition and inciting the people to rebel against Rome (Luke 23:1-2).

TRIAL BEFORE PILATE

The most famous trial in all history began on the day we now call Good Friday. Very little is known about Pontius Pilate before he was appointed Governor or Procurator of Judea by the Emperor Tiberius in 26 AD. As the Procurator, he had control of the province and was in charge of the army that occupied Israel. Pilate had full power of life and death, and could reverse any capital sentence passed by the Sanhedrin. Every sentence handed down by the Sanhedrin court had to be submitted to the Governor for ratification. The Governor also had the authority to appoint the high priests as well as control of the Temple and its funds. The vestments of the high priest were in his custody and these vestments were released only for festivals, when the Procurator took up residence in Jerusalem. The historian Josephus records that on taking up his appointment in Judea, Pilate's first action in placing Roman standards in the city of Jerusalem antagonized the Jews. Previous Procurators had avoided using these standards in Jerusalem, as they bore images of the Emperor. The people resisted Pilate's actions, even at the threat of death. Six days later, the standards were removed and taken to Caesarea. This was not Pilate's only offence against the Jews. He also used money from the Temple treasury to build an aqueduct to bring water forty kilometres to the city. Thousands of Jews demonstrated against this project and Pilate disguised his troops and sent them in amongst the crowds, so that many lost their lives. Some consider that this riot may be the one mentioned in Luke chapter 13, where Pilate may have had some Galileans killed while they were offering their daily sacrifices in the temple.[12]

The New Testament intimates that Pilate was a weak man, ready to serve with expediency rather than with principle. He is remembered in both religious and secular history as the man who authorized the death of Jesus Christ. In Christian churches where the "Nicene Creed" or "Apostles' Creed" are upheld as doctrinal statements of faith, worshippers are reminded week after week that we worship a crucified Messiah: *Christ was crucified under Pontius Pilate, suffered, died and was buried.* Although Pilate could find no basis for a charge against Jesus, he eventually ordered His crucifixion. He did so to please the Jewish authorities and to maintain his relationship with Caiaphas, his appointed high priest. All four Gospels record that Jesus stood before Pilate for judgment, but they differ slightly in describing this trial. All four Gospels though, consistently state that Pilate tried to find some way to set Jesus free. If anything shocked Pilate, it was Jesus' refusal to respond to the charges made against Him.

According to Mark's Gospel, Pilate knew that the Chief Priests, because of envy, handed Jesus over to him for judgment, and so he looked for a way to release Jesus (Mark 15:9). In fact, the

Scriptures state that Pilate attempted to release Jesus on four separate occasions.

As recorded in John's Gospel, Pilate's first attempt to set Jesus free occurred when Pilate wanted to turn Jesus over to the Jewish authorities. He urged them to judge Jesus by their own laws. They responded that they would not have turned Jesus over to Pilate if He were not a criminal. They accused Jesus of making Himself out to be a king. It is clear from the Gospels that Pilate did not ever see Jesus as a threat to Roman authority. Although Jesus did not deny being a king, He acknowledged that His kingdom was not of this world. After Pilate heard this testimony of kingship, he returned to the Jewish authorities and advised them that there was no basis for charges against Jesus and that he desired to release Him.

Luke the historian recorded Pilate's second attempt to release Jesus in his Gospel. When Pilate discovered that Jesus was a Galilean, he turned Him over to King Herod for judgment. Pilate could do this since Jesus, as a Galilean, was rightfully under Herod's jurisdiction. As the ruler of Galilee, Herod was not under the same pressure to please the High Priest or the Sanhedrin. When Jesus stood before him, Herod's prime concern was to have Him perform a miracle. Although Herod plied him with many questions, and the priests and teachers of the law vehemently accused Him, Jesus made no response. Herod's soldiers mocked and ridiculed Jesus and then dressed him in an elegant robe and sent him back to Pilate.

Pilate's third attempt to release Jesus came about because of a Roman custom: *"Now it was the governor's custom at the Feast to release a prisoner chosen by the crowd. At the time they had a notorious prisoner, called Barabbas"* (Matthew 27:15-16). Barabbas had committed murder and was in prison with the insurrectionists. Pilate asked the crowd, *"Which one do you want me to release to you: Barabbas, or Jesus who is called the Christ?"* (Matthew 27:17b). The crowd, incited by the teachers of the law, asked for Barabbas and for Pilate to order Jesus' crucifixion.

John the Apostle records Pilate's fourth and last attempt to release Jesus:

> *Then Pilate took Jesus and had him flogged. The soldiers twisted together a crown of thorns and put it on his head. They clothed him in a purple robe and went up to him again and again saying, "Hail, King of the Jews!" And they struck him in the face. Once more Pilate came out and said to the Jews, "Look, I am bringing him out to you to let you know that I find no basis for a charge against him." When Jesus came out wearing the crown of thorns and the purple robe, Pilate said to them, "Here is the man!"* (John 19:1-5)

Even though Jesus had not been found guilty of any crime, He had been scourged, mocked and ridiculed by Pilate's soldiers. Pilate may have been trying to invoke sympathy for Jesus from the crowd in allowing this. After all this punishment, Jesus did not look like a king. He looked like a man who had been whipped and beaten to within an inch of His life. How could this broken and bruised man any longer be a threat to anyone? Yet the crowd was relentless in its desire to have Pilate order the crucifixion of Jesus.

With cries of *"Crucify him, Crucify him,"* ringing in his ears, Pilate once again suggested that the Jewish rulers crucify Jesus, as he could not help but find Him innocent of all charges. In an act of desperation, the Jewish rulers brought to Pilate's attention the real reason they had set Jesus before him. *"We have a law and according to that law, he must die, because he claimed to be the Son of God"* (John 19:7). Pilate questioned Jesus again, and informed Him that he had the authority to set Him free or to crucify Him. Jesus responded that Pilate had no authority except that which had been given him from above. John's Gospel says that from that time on, Pilate did his utmost to release Jesus. The crowd once again changed tactics though, and accused Pilate of being an enemy of Caesar.

The very last thing that Pilate did was to insult the crowd, the Jewish leaders and the teachers of the law. He did this by adopting a ritual out of Jewish law. When a person has been murdered and the killer cannot be identified, the elders of the community gather and having sacrificed a heifer, wash their hands over the sacrifice and then declare, *"Our hands did not shed this blood, nor did our eyes see it done. Accept this atonement for your people Israel, whom you have redeemed, O Lord, and do not hold your people guilty of the blood of an innocent man"* (Deuteronomy 21:6-8). Pilate was aware, as he performed this ritual known as the "washing of the hands," that it should be carried out only in cases of murder. The crowd understood, for they cried out to Pilate, *"Let his blood be on us and on our children"* (Matthew 27:25). Pilate then ordered the crucifixion of Jesus. Although Pilate made every attempt to set Jesus free, he is no less culpable for His death. He had the authority and the power to reverse the findings of the court of the Sanhedrin, but he chose to order the death of an innocent man.

We now have a fuller understanding of how Jesus came to be crucified. In summary: Judas, His good friend and close disciple, betrayed Him to the priests for thirty pieces of silver. After a mock trial the priests turned Him over to Pilate. The charge against him in their court was one of blasphemy. He had claimed to be the Son of God and had threatened to destroy their holy temple—and so at best, he had to be an impostor and at worst, a blasphemer. These leaders looked for the Messiah whose coming had been foretold by the Old Testament prophets, one who would be a powerful Jewish King, who would conquer the enemies of the chosen people and deliver them from Roman occupation. To their minds, Jesus was just the opposite of what they wanted. He was humble and meek. He taught people to love their enemies and to do good to those who hated them. He was a friend of sinners, publicans and the social outcasts of His day. He exposed the hypocrisy of the religious leaders. In so doing, He undermined the prestige of those who considered themselves the pillars of Jewish national and religious interests. To these Jewish leaders, Jesus was a social outcast, a political renegade and a heretic who had to be stopped. They could not prove him guilty of heresy or blasphemy in their court, yet they pronounced Him guilty and intended that He should die. When they turned Jesus over to Pilate, in order to secure a death sentence they changed the offences from religious to political by accusing Him of sedition against Rome. Pilate, to avoid another major riot, handed Jesus over to the soldiers to be crucified.

Why couldn't the Lord of Creation, the One who healed the sick, opened the eyes of the blind, preached the Good News of God's love to thousands, raised the dead and even walked on water—He who performed all these miracles—why couldn't He still the voices clamouring for His death? There was no doubt that He had the power and authority. The night before, when Jesus was arrested, He told the crowd that He could call upon His Father: *"Do you think I cannot call on my Father, and he will at once put at my disposal more than twelve legions of angels? But how then would the Scriptures be fulfilled that say it must happen this way?"* (Matthew 26:53). But the angels were not summoned and in spite of their promises of loyalty, the disciples ran away in fear. Jesus was arrested, tried in an improperly constituted religious hearing, declared innocent in a court of law, and was crucified.

Was He a martyr dying to uphold His cause? *Absolutely not!* According to the biblical record, Jesus went to the cross by His own deliberate choice and in accordance with His Father's pre-set plan. This was no accident. In chapter 2 of Acts, we read that Peter and the Eleven, having been baptized with the Holy Spirit, stood in front of the crowd on the Day of Pentecost. Peter delivered the first of the messages that were to become common in the early church. He made it known to the crowd quite clearly that it was through God's plan that Jesus was handed over to wicked men to be put to death by them.

"Men of Israel, listen to this: Jesus of Nazareth was a man accredited by God to you by miracles, wonders and signs, which God did among you through him, as you yourselves know. This man was

handed over to you by God's set purpose and foreknowledge; and you, with the help of wicked men, put him to death by nailing him to the cross." (Acts 2:22-23)

In the rest of this chapter we need to look at God's plan of salvation, the reasons why Jesus had to die, and the benefits for humanity achieved by Jesus' death on the Cross of Redemption.

GOD'S PLAN OF SALVATION

To be quite clear, Jesus' death on the cross was *not* God's emergency plan. God did not make our world and rest on the seventh day to come back on the eighth day and find the world in a mess. The most amazing thing about the death of Jesus was that it was planned *even* before the foundation of the world was laid down. Astonishing? Absolutely! That is what the Scriptures tell us.

In writing about our salvation, Peter said:

For you know that it was not with perishable things such as silver or gold that you were redeemed from the empty way of life handed down to you from your forefathers, but with the precious blood of Christ, a lamb without blemish or defect. He was chosen before the creation of the world, but was revealed in these last times for your sake. (1 Peter 1:18-20, emphasis added)

Paul also wrote:

For he chose us in him before the creation of the world to be holy and blameless in his sight. In love he predestined us to be adopted as his sons through Jesus Christ, in accordance with his pleasure and will, to the praise of his glorious grace, which he has freely given us in the One he loves. In him we have redemption through his blood, the forgiveness of sins, in accordance with the riches of God's grace that he lavished on us with all wisdom and understanding. (Ephesians 1:4-8)

The last book of the Bible speaks to us of the names written in God's book of life, for they belong to the *"Lamb that was slain from the creation of the world"* (Revelation 13:8).

Even before God spoke the world into being, it was His plan that His Son would die for the redemption of the world. Does anyone truly understand why? No! The love of God is in many ways beyond human comprehension and the cross of Jesus will always remain an enigma. What we do know for sure is that God loves us so much that even before we fell into sin and turned our backs on Him and hid, He already had a plan that would bring us home. In his book, *Watchers by the Cross,* the Rev. Peter Green included this description of the cross:

> What is the Cross, but the candle set by our Heavenly Father's hand in the window, to shine out through the darkness of sin and shame, to guide us back to the Father's house, and to say to the wandering soul: 'Come back, my child, come back.' And the soul, seeing it, takes heart to creep back, trembling, and to unlatch that door which is never bolted nor barred, and to find forgiveness and peace in our true home.[13]

Many have grown up at a time when the cross was seen only as a symbol of pain and sorrow. I don't remember ever hearing that the Father sent the Son to die on a cross because of love. The cross of Jesus haunted me as a child. Each week when I went to church, a massive crucifix hanging in the centre of the Sanctuary confronted me. In the eyes of this child that cross seemed to be nine feet tall and six feet wide. The bloody wounds were dramatized by red paint that seemed to flow endlessly from the body on the cross. Blood from the wounds caused by the crown of thorns on His head, blood from the wounds on His hands and feet, blood from His side, blood everywhere. The wounds were so raw, and life-like, they overwhelmed me. The eyes staring down haunted me and followed me into every corner, and I felt trapped, helpless and hopeless. I railed against that cross and the man who hung there, and told God that it wasn't my fault. It was His fault! I had been told that God killed His Son for the sins of the world and in particular, had killed Him because of the evil in my heart.

If that wasn't enough to turn my heart to stone, how could I live with the guilt imposed by the teaching that my sins were driving the nails deeper and deeper into Jesus' body? If God was so powerful and mighty, He could have changed the hearts of all people and His Son wouldn't have had to die. For years I prayed that God would make me good enough to stop causing that man upon the cross so much pain. I was convinced that God could have made me righteous, holy and obedient. Instead, He permitted me to rebel and to turn my back on Him, as He had turned His back on His Son. Yes, there was a small part of me that wanted to embrace the cross, but the pain and grief displayed there were too much. I wanted to receive the forgiveness being offered, but the hardness in my heart forced me to run from that cross. Running was easier and so, for twenty-six years I ran. Eventually I grew weary and one night, the cross overcame me. When I finally looked at the cross as if through the eyes of the Father and with the understanding of Scripture, I discovered for the first time the grace and the love that the cross brings into our lives. Once again I turn to John Stott in *The Cross of Christ* to illustrate the grievous damage that can be done to others because of half-truths. Stott writes:

> How could anyone imagine that Christianity is about sin rather than about the forgiveness of sin? How could anyone look at the cross and see only the shame of what we did to Christ, rather than the glory of what he did for us? The prodigal son had to 'come to himself' (acknowledge his self-centeredness) before he could 'come home to his father'.
>
> The humiliation of penitence was necessary before the joy of reconciliation. There would have been no ring, no robe, no kiss, and no feast if he had remained in the far country or returned impenitent. A guilty conscience is a great blessing, but only if it drives us to come home.[14]

One of my primary goals as a pastor is to help others know that the Cross of Redemption is God's solution to our lostness and to our sins. The Cross of Redemption is the gateway or the bridge that will lead us home to the Father. There is no doubt that for Jesus the Cross of Redemption was a place of pain, grief and grave suffering. But to those who are being redeemed and made right with God, it is there that we begin to see the Father's love. At the front of this book, I have quoted the words of Octavius Winslow:

WHO DELIVERED UP JESUS TO DIE?
NOT JUDAS, FOR MONEY;
NOT PILATE, FOR FEAR;
NOT THE JEWS, FOR ENVY;
BUT THE FATHER, FOR LOVE.[15]

Yes, it was for love that the Father sent Jesus into this world to die. Jesus died for each one of us out of love. An unknown author wrote: "Jesus, how much do you love me?" "This much," he replied, and stretched out his arms and died."

I have already shared with you that most familiar verse in all Scripture *"God so loved the world that he gave his one and only Son…"* (John 3:16). In his letter to the Romans, Paul brings us what I would call an awesome description of God's love. No matter how many times I read this passage, I am overwhelmed by Paul's depiction of God's love for each of us.

If God is for us, who can be against us? He who did not spare his own Son, but gave him up for us all—how will he not also, along with him, graciously give us all things? Who will bring any charge against those whom God has chosen? It is God who justifies. Who is he that condemns? Christ Jesus, who died—more than that, who was raised to life—is at the right hand of God and is also interceding for us. Who shall separate us from the love of Christ? Shall trouble or hardship or persecution or famine or nakedness or danger or sword? As it is written: "For your sake we face death all day long;

we are considered as sheep to be slaughtered." No, in all these things we are more than conquerors through him who loved us. For I am convinced that neither death nor life, neither angels nor demons, neither the present nor the future, nor any powers, neither height nor depth, nor anything else in all creation, will be able to separate us from the love of God that is in Christ Jesus our Lord. (Romans 8:31b-39)

This passage of Scripture is for you. It tells you that God is on your side. That God is aware of your situation. You may have to go through difficult trials and tribulations, but absolutely nothing can ever separate you from His love, care and compassion for you, His precious child. Also know that, as you go through trials and tribulations, there is an intercessor in heaven constantly praying for your situation. While intercession includes prayer, it also includes the clear idea of someone representing us in another realm. That intercessor is none other than our Lord and Saviour Jesus Christ. At times you may wonder at God's love and care for you, but this has been written: "If you were the only one, Jesus Christ would come and die for you."

WHY DID JESUS HAVE TO DIE?

The simple answer is that Jesus Christ came into this world with the purpose of dying for humanity. Although some are shocked that He was crucified on the cross, He is not shocked—He knew He came to die. The theologian P.T. Forsyth states: "The Cross was not simply a fate awaiting Christ in the future; it pervaded subliminally his holy Person. He was born for the cross. It was his genius, his destiny."[16] I said earlier, the golden thread that runs through the Gospel of Luke is God's message of salvation for the world. This message of salvation is not a hidden one but is conveyed on every page of the Gospel. The angel Gabriel tells Mary that she will give birth to God's Son and they are to give Him the name Jesus (Luke 1:31). Jesus means, *Jehovah is salvation* or *Yahweh saves*. When the angels come to the shepherds, they are told that a Saviour has been born for them. When Jesus is presented at the temple, Mary is told: *"This child is destined to cause the falling and rising of many in Israel and to be a sign that will be spoken against, so that the thoughts of many hearts will be revealed. And a sword will pierce your own soul too"* (Luke 2:34-35).

Luke is the only Gospel writer to tell us any stories about Jesus' childhood. When Jesus was twelve years old, the family went to Jerusalem for the Feast of the Passover. When Mary and Joseph were traveling home, they realized that Jesus was not with them. On returning to Jerusalem, they found Him in the temple. *"Why were you searching for me?"* he asked. *"Didn't you know I had to be in my Father's house?"* (Luke 2:49). Although some current theologians speculate and disagree, I believe that Jesus knew His purpose from the very beginning of His life. Although the cross is not mentioned in any of the above references, Jesus didn't come into the world to be a great teacher or miracle worker. Although teaching and miracles were part of His ministry, His goal was the salvation of the world. This was marked out from the beginning of His ministry. He came as *"the Lamb of God"* (John 1:29) to bear our sins in His body and thereby set us free from death. His first act of ministry was to undergo baptism. As the sinless Lamb of God, He did not need to be baptized, but He did so to identify Himself with sinners He came to save. After baptism, He went into the desert for forty days where He was tempted by the devil. Would He be deflected from the way of the cross? He was offered a way out, but in obedience to His Father, He steadfastly refused to go the way of the world, the flesh or the devil.

As Jesus began His ministry, He gathered His disciples around Him, although the primary purpose of His ministry was not yet clear to these men. They were caught up with Jesus' teaching, His miracles and His fellowship. The changing point of Jesus' ministry took place at Caesarea Philippi. It was there where Jesus made His purpose clear. Caesarea Philippi was the birthplace of the 'gods.' "In ancient history, the city gained its fame as the centre for Baal worship...According to

Greek mythology, the birth of Pan—the god of nature—took place in a cave from which sprang the waters of the Jordan River."[17] It was in this setting, surrounded by all these so-called "gods," that Jesus asked the question that defined the direction of His ministry, *"Who do you say that I am?"* (Mark 8:29). It was Simon Peter who answered, *"You are the Christ"* (Mark 8:30). The Greek title, "the Christ" and the Hebrew/Aramaic "the Messiah" carry the same meaning: "Anointed One." The implication is that one so titled has been selected by God to fulfil a particular task (for example, the Jewish kings and the priests of the Old Testament). In making such selections, God gave not only the tasks but also the special powers and abilities required to accomplish the task. Over time, many Jews had narrowed down their understanding and expectations of one so selected by God to be a Saviour of the people from those who oppressed them—one who would bring back the glory days they had known under King David—a "Son of David" who would be their Saviour.[18]

When Peter confessed that Jesus was "the Christ," Jesus made no attempt to deny what he had said, but He warned them not to tell others (Mark 8:30b). The reason for this was that there were some who looked upon the Messiah as a political figure who would come to set the Israelites free from Rome. Immediately after this confession, Jesus revealed to these followers His purpose as "the Christ":

> *He then began to teach them that the Son of Man must suffer many things and be rejected by the elders, chief priests and teachers of the law, and that he must be killed and after three days rise again. He spoke plainly about this...* (Mark 8:31-32)

Jesus' announcement to the disciples must have been an overwhelming shock. A distraught Peter pulled Jesus aside and remonstrated with Him. As recorded in Matthew's Gospel, Jesus earlier had praised Peter for his unhesitating acknowledgement of Him as "the Christ" (Matthew 16:17-19), but now he found himself rebuked by Jesus: *"But when Jesus turned and looked at his disciples, he rebuked Peter. 'Get behind me, Satan!' he said. 'You do not have in mind the things of God, but the things of men'*" (Mark 8:33). The first word of rebuke was reminiscent of Jesus' rebuke to Satan in the desert (Luke 4:1-13). The second part of the rebuke told Peter that he was no different from many others who were looking for an earthly military or political redeemer. Jesus had been very clear that God's Messiah would bring liberation through death and resurrection, not via armies or military victories. Jesus continued that if anyone was ashamed of Him and His words, the day would come when the Son of Man will return and will be ashamed of them (Mark 8:38). I have called this the turning point of Jesus' ministry, for it is here where He announced that the *cross* was His purpose in life.

Almost twenty-one centuries later, we still stumble over this cross. Many want a "Christ" without a cross. We want a teacher, a miracle-worker, a social worker, but not a suffering servant. We want a "Christ" who will serve us, but not one who suffers for us. For we know that it is for *us* that He suffers. From this moment on in Jesus' ministry, the theme of the suffering servant becomes clear. Shortly after this encounter in Philippi, Jesus told the disciples even more plainly,

> *"We are going up to Jerusalem," he said, "and the Son of Man will be betrayed to the chief priests and teachers of the law. They will condemn him to death and will hand him over to the Gentiles, who will mock him and spit on him, flog him and kill him. Three days later he will rise." (Mark 10:33-34)*

It is obvious from Mark's Gospel that the disciples still did not understand, because after this proclamation James and John came to Him and asked for a special place in heaven. So once more Jesus said, *"The Son of Man did not come to be served, but to serve, and to give his life as a ransom for many"* (Mark 10:45). By offering Himself as a ransom, Jesus declared Himself to be the Redeemer of Humanity.

JESUS THE REDEEMER

Slavery was a common practice in the ancient world. Since many Jewish people had slaves they were well aware of the impact of the relationship of slave to master and master to slave. They were well aware that a slave could be ransomed, or redeemed by a monetary settlement. In a confrontation described by John in his Gospel (John 8:31-46), Jesus tells the Pharisees that they were not true children of Abraham as they claimed, but, because they were enslaved by sin, were in fact children of the devil. Jesus told this audience that He came to set them free from slavery and would pay the price of redemption. Paul, more than any other writer, makes the most of this theology of redemption in his Epistles.

In Ephesians he tells us that, "*In Christ, we have redemption through his blood, the forgiveness of sins*" (Ephesians 1:7). In Romans he writes that we are, "*justified freely by his grace through the redemption that came by Christ Jesus*" (Romans 3:24). Also in Romans he refers to the future redemption of our bodies, "*...we ourselves, who have the firstfruits of the Spirit, groan inwardly as we wait eagerly for our adoption as sons, the redemption of our bodies*" (Romans 8:23). In Colossians he reminds us that, "*Christ has rescued us from the dominion of darkness and brought us into the kingdom of the Son he loves, in whom we have redemption, the forgiveness of sins*" (Colossians 1:13-14). In Galatians, he tells us that we have also been set free from the curse of the law that we could not keep, "*Christ redeemed us from the curse of the law by becoming a curse for us, for it is written: 'Cursed is everyone who is hung on a tree.'*" (Galatians 3:13).

In the above passages Paul demonstrates that Jesus accomplished for us something that we could not accomplish for ourselves. Paul not only proclaims that Jesus has redeemed us, but the purchase price of that redemption was the precious blood of Jesus.

This theme of redemption and its cost is not restricted to Paul's writing but can also be found in Peter's First Epistle:

For you know that it was not with perishable things such as silver or gold that you were redeemed from the empty way of life handed down to you from your forefathers, but with the precious blood of Christ, a lamb without blemish or defect. (1 Peter 1:18-19)

Later in this Epistle, Peter speaks of the suffering that Christians endure because of persecution and reminds us of what Jesus has accomplished for us:

He himself bore our sins in his body on the tree, so that we might die to sins and live for righteousness; by his wounds you have been healed. For you were like sheep going astray, but now you have returned to the Shepherd and Overseer of your souls. (1 Peter 2: 24-25)

The writer to the Hebrews has also affirmed this theme of redemption. This letter was written to Jewish Christians who, under the threat of persecution, were being tempted to renounce Jesus and revert to Judaism. John Stott in *The Cross of Christ* writes:

The author's tactic was to demonstrate the supremacy of Jesus Christ, not only as Son over the angels and as Prophet over Moses, but in particular as Priest over the now obsolete Levitical priesthood. For the sacrificial ministry of Jesus our 'great high priest' (Hebrews 4:14), is incomparably superior to theirs. He had no sins of his own for which to make sacrifice; the blood he shed was not of goats and calves, but his own; he had no need to offer the same sacrifices repeatedly, which could never take away sins, because he made 'one sacrifice for sins for ever'; and he has thus obtained an 'eternal redemption' and established an 'eternal covenant' which contains the promise, 'I will forgive their wickedness and remember their sins no more.' (Hebrews 8:10)

The last book of the Bible has also proclaimed this theme of redemption. In Revelation, Jesus is referred to as the *'Lamb'* twenty-eight times. This designation rightly belongs to Jesus because He offered Himself as a sacrifice and with His blood He has purchased humanity's salvation. This redemption of Christ is without restriction, for Jesus has redeemed people of every gender, language, race and nation:

> *You are worthy to take the scroll and to open its seals, because you were slain, and with your blood you purchased men for God from every tribe and language and people and nation. You have made them to be a kingdom and priests to serve our God, and they will reign on the earth. Then I looked and heard the voice of many angels, numbering thousands upon thousands, and ten thousand times ten thousand. They encircled the throne and the living creatures and the elders. In a loud voice they sang: "Worthy is the Lamb, who was slain, to receive power and wealth and wisdom and strength and honour and glory and praise!"* (Revelation 5:9-12)

In Revelation, John emphasized that Jesus, as the Lamb of God who was slain, will triumph in heaven and for all eternity.

Redemption not only looks back to Calvary Hill, but also forward to the freedom in which the "redeemed of the Lord" are to stand. Paul says to the church in Corinth: *"... you were bought at a price. Therefore honour God with your body"* (1 Corinthians 6:20). We must show that we are people who have moved from being enslaved to sin to freedom in Jesus. We do this by showing the fruit of God's Holy Spirit in our lives, the fruits of love, joy, peace, patience, kindness, goodness, faithfulness, gentleness and self-control (Galatians 5:22-25).

Let us see now how Jesus' life laid down on the cross opened the door to reconciliation and ended humanity's alienation from God that had existed ever since the events in the Garden—how the death of Jesus the Redeemer benefited all humanity.

RECONCILIATION WITH GOD

Paul writes: *"Once you were alienated from God and were enemies in your minds because of your evil behaviour. But now he has reconciled you by Christ's physical body through death to present you holy in his sight, without blemish and without accusation"* (Colossians 1:21-22). Prior to Jesus' death, humanity was alienated from God. This alienation began in the Garden and carried on until the death of Jesus. Although the nation of Israel was God's chosen people and entered into covenants with Him, those were limited covenants. The sacrifices and offerings to God were carried out in an earthly sanctuary. The writer to the Hebrews says that this earthly sanctuary was only a copy and a shadow of what was in heaven. In the earthly sanctuary, a tabernacle was set up:

> *In its first room were the lampstand, the table and the consecrated bread; this was called the Holy Place. Behind the second curtain was a room called the Most Holy Place, which had the golden altar of incense and the gold-covered ark of the covenant. This ark contained the gold jar of manna, Aaron's staff that had budded, and the stone tablets of the covenant.* (Hebrews 9:2-4)

The only person who was allowed to go into the Most Holy Place was the High Priest and then only once a year. He could never go in without offering a blood sacrifice for his sins and those of the people he represented. When Jesus died on Calvary Hill on Good Friday, the synoptic Gospels all record that the curtain in the temple was supernaturally torn from top to bottom (Matthew 27:51; Mark 15: 38; Luke 23:15). Why? Again the writer to the Hebrews gives us this answer:

> *When Christ came as high priest of the good things that are already here, he went through the greater and more perfect tabernacle that is not man-made, that is to say, not a part of this creation. He did not enter by means of the blood of goats and calves; but he entered the Most Holy Place once for all by his own blood, having obtained eternal redemption. The blood of goats and bulls and the ashes of a heifer sprinkled on those who are ceremonially unclean sanctify them so that they are outwardly clean. How much more, then, will the blood of Christ, who through the eternal Spirit offered himself*

unblemished to God, cleanse our consciences from acts that lead to death, so that we may serve the living God. (Hebrews 9:11-14)

At the moment the curtain was torn, we were granted access into God's presence. We were reconciled. Jesus as our High Priest reconciled us to God. Earlier in Hebrews we find:

Therefore, since we have a great high priest who has gone through the heavens, Jesus the Son of God, let us hold firmly to the faith we profess. For we do not have a high priest who is unable to sympathize with our weaknesses, but we have one who has been tempted in every way, just as we are—yet was without sin. Let us then approach the throne of grace with confidence, so that we may receive mercy and find grace to help us in our time of need. (Hebrews 4:14-16)

This reconciliation is not our work, but God's work, and it was achieved only through Jesus' death. In his letter to the Colossians, Paul wrote: *"For God was pleased to have all his fullness dwell in him (in Christ) and through him to reconcile to himself all things; whether things on earth or things in heaven, by making peace through his blood, shed on the cross"* (Colossians 1:19-20). This reconciliation is not a process to be worked out; it is an act of God by which He has delivered humanity from sin and death. The Church has been entrusted with the responsibility of sharing this news of reconciliation with those who are outside the kingdom of God: *"All this is from God, who reconciled us to himself through Christ and gave us the ministry of reconciliation: that God was reconciling the world to himself in Christ, not counting men's sins against them. And he has committed to us the message of reconciliation"* (2 Corinthians 5:18-19).

As the Church we are entrusted with telling the world that God has intervened in our world—not to punish rebellious subjects, but to reconcile us with Himself. He wants to show Himself not as our enemy, but as our friend. It is an illusion to think that God is our enemy or is indifferent to any one of us. He has always been and always will be our Heavenly Father, who desires not the death of sinners, but the reconciliation of sinners in the name of His Son. All of this was accomplished in the life, work and death of Jesus Christ.

JUSTIFICATION BEFORE GOD

In order to understand what it means to be "justified before God," we have to look at what makes us "unjustified" or "condemned" before God. In Romans, Paul is very clear about the state of humanity: "*There is no one righteous, not even one*" (Romans 3:10) and, "*For all have sinned and fall short of the glory of God*" (Romans 3:23). The word *sin* is not a popular word in this day and age. For many the word *sin* is archaic, belonging to a previous generation. If I were to compare this time in history with a biblical period, I would pick the period of the Judges.

After the Israelites moved into the Promised Land, their leader Joshua and those of his generation died. The Scriptures say:

> *After that whole generation had been gathered to their fathers, another generation grew up, who knew neither the Lord nor what he had done for Israel. Then the Israelites did evil in the eyes of the Lord…they forsook the Lord, the God of their fathers who had brought them out of Egypt. They followed and worshiped various gods of the people around them…in his anger against Israel the Lord handed them over to raiders who plundered them. He sold them to their enemies all around, whom they were no longer able to resist…they were in great distress.* (Judges 2:10-15)

The book of Judges is an account of the nation of Israel frequently falling away from God and as a result is sold into slavery and subjected to harsh rulers. It also tells of the nation's urgent petitions to God in times of crisis. The Lord responded again and again by raising up leaders (judges) who threw off the oppressors, brought peace to the land and turned the people back to worshiping the God who rescued them from Egypt. Throughout this book there are recurring cycles of apostasy, oppression, distress and deliverance. The book closes with the words, *"Everyone did as he saw fit"* (Judges 21:25), or as the King James Version puts it, *"Every man did that which was right in his own eyes."* That last statement describes the state of today's world. Sin is no longer recognized as sin. Lifestyles are seen as "choices" and one choice is as good as another. The holiness of God and the majesty of God have been set aside. If there is an image of God, it is that of a benevolent grandfather-like figure who is tolerant of any behaviour. That image of God, however, is not compatible with the scriptural image of a holy God. The holiness of God is one of the foundation stones of biblical religion. Sin is incompatible with God's holiness—God's eyes are too pure to look on evil and He cannot tolerate wrong (Habakkuk 1:13).

According to the biblical record, humanity has a "sin problem" and God is the only one who can deal with that predicament. All forgiveness begins with God. Why? God was the first to be sinned against. God is also the first to offer a way of reconciliation for that sin and all the sins that followed. The familiar story of the fall of humanity occurs in chapter 3 of Genesis. The only thing God forbade—they did. Some people who read this story in Genesis think that Adam and Eve ate a piece of fruit and God over-reacted. This story is not about a piece of fruit. It is there to tell us of a separation that occurred between God and humanity because of sin. It's a story about betrayal, disobedience, rebellion, and usurping the authority of God. It's a story about humanity turning its back on God. Sin cannot gaze into the holy face of God. God cannot gaze into the face of sin without destroying it. Immediately after this fall, God made a promise that one day He would provide a way in which humanity could be reconciled with Him (Genesis 3:15). Like so many today, Adam and Eve tried to deal with their sin in their own way, and that is why they covered themselves with fig leaves. But the fig leaves couldn't cleanse or remove the sin, which is why they felt 'ashamed' and why they ran and hid from God. When God discovered where they were hiding,

He handed out the appropriate punishment, but He also promised future redemption from their sin. As well, before they were banished from the Garden, God provided them with clothing as an adequate cover for their sins: *"The Lord God made garments of skin for Adam and his wife and clothed them"* (Genesis 3:21). In order for Adam and Eve's sin to be "covered" an animal had to be sacrificed.

As we read through the Old Testament, we see how God introduced the sacrificial rite of atonement to His people. The word atonement means *"a-making-at-one,"* so that those who are estranged from each other are brought back into unity with each other. This atonement is always linked to sacrifice. As the sacrifice occurs, the sin is lifted or removed from the sinner and forgiveness is received. God implemented the sacrificial system of atonement through Moses. Forgiveness is only possible because God is a God of grace, or as Nehemiah puts it, God is a forgiving God. *"But you are a forgiving God, gracious and compassionate, slow to anger and abounding in love"* (Nehemiah 9:17). Much of the language and imagery used in the Old Testament speaks of God's forgiving nature and is there to give us the assurance of His total forgiveness. It is not hard to see that forgiveness is rooted in the nature of God. When God forgives, sins are no longer seen or remembered.

The one thing about the sacrificial system of the Old Testament however, is that the sins could be covered but, as the writer to the Hebrews reminds us, they could not be removed: *"But those sacrifices are an annual reminder of sins, because it is impossible for the blood of bulls and goats to take away sins"* (Hebrews 10:4). It is when we turn to the New Testament we find that sins are not merely covered—they are permanently removed: *"Behold, the Lamb of God, who takes away the sin of the world"* (John 1:29).

In the New Testament, we find that the word forgiveness means, "deal graciously with" or "send away." The New Testament differs from the Old though, in that it insists that, in order to be forgiven, a sinner must also forgive. Our readiness to forgive others is a part indication that we have truly repented. We forgive others not because of our charity, but because Jesus has forgiven us. Where do we go to find that forgiveness? There is only one place, and that is to the Cross: *"In Him, we have redemption through His blood, the forgiveness of our sins"* (Ephesians 1:7). The new covenant that Jesus instituted on the night He was betrayed is based on these words, *"This is my blood of the covenant, which is poured out for many for the forgiveness of sins."* (Matthew 26:28) Forgiveness rests solely on the atoning work of Jesus, and is a sheer act of grace: *"He is faithful and just and will forgive our sins"* (1 John 1:9).

We need to bear in mind that forgiveness does not stand alone. It stands side by side with faith. It is by faith and repentance that we come to Jesus, and it is in Jesus and through Jesus that we are able to appropriate the grace of God. Sin and grace go together. If we speak of sin without mentioning grace, we dishonour Jesus' sacrifice on the cross and we end up with a distorted image of God. If we speak of grace without mentioning sin, we dishonour Jesus' sacrifice and cheapen the message of the Gospel. The Church of Jesus Christ has no Good News to preach without the crucifixion. Jesus did not come to earth to die for our mistakes or for the weaknesses of our flesh. Instead He came to die for *sin*. Sin is the human will colliding with the divine will. It's about an ego that is bent on rebellion, hatred, disobedience and indifference to the price God was willing to pay for our salvation.

Before we can truly appreciate the forgiveness of God, we have to admit that we need His forgiveness. The most unpopular topic that a preacher or a writer can discuss is sin as they are fully aware that they are also caught in the trap of sin. It may appear to others that they are judging or condemning and as a result one must approach the topic with sensitivity and gentleness.

According to the Scriptures, sin is a state of being alienated from God, from others and even from ourselves. We do not wish to admit that we are sinners and resent being told that we are sinners because our concept and understanding of sin is basically flawed. We agree that the thief, the drunkard, the murderer, the adulterer and the molester are guilty sinners in need of punishment. Good people don't live like that. They live decent, ordinary, hard-working, tax-paying lives. They are never in danger of going to court, or prison, or getting their names in the paper for the wrong reasons. Therefore, sin has nothing to do with them. That is not true.

Allow me to tell you in his words the story of the American pastor, John Wimber, who had a great influence in North America from the late seventies to the early nineties. John readily admits that he did not consider himself much of a sinner, nor did he fully comprehend the purpose of the cross. However, in his book, *Equipping the Saints*, he tells the story of his encounter with the cross, an encounter that changed his life.

After I had studied the Bible ... for about three months, I could have passed an elementary exam on the cross. I understood there is one God who could be known in three Persons. I understood Jesus is fully God and fully man and he died on the cross for the sins of the world. But I didn't understand that I was a sinner. I thought I was a good guy. I knew I messed up here and there but I didn't realize how serious my condition was. But one evening around this time Carol, my wife, said, "I think it's time to do something about all that we've been learning." Then, as I looked on in utter amazement, she knelt down on the floor and started praying to what seemed to me to be the ceiling plaster. "Oh God," she said, "I am sorry for my sin." I couldn't believe it. Carol was a better person than I, yet she thought she was a sinner. I could feel her pain and the depth of her prayers. Soon she was weeping and repeating, "I am sorry for my sin." There were six or seven people in the room, all with their eyes closed. I looked at them and then it hit me: They've all prayed this prayer too! I started sweating bullets. I thought I was going to die. The perspiration ran down my face and I thought, "I'm not going to do this. This is dumb. I'm a good guy." Then it struck me. Carol wasn't praying to the plaster; she was praying to a person, to a God who could hear her. In comparison to him she knew she was a sinner in need of forgiveness.

In a flash the cross made personal sense to me. Suddenly I knew something that I had never known before; I had hurt God's feelings. He loved me and in his love for me he sent Jesus. But I had turned away from that love; I had shunned it all of my life. I was a sinner, desperately in need of the cross. Then I too was kneeling on the floor, sobbing, nose running, eyes watering, every square inch of my flesh perspiring profusely. I had this overwhelming sense that I was talking with someone who had been with me all of my life, but whom I failed to recognize. Like Carol, I began talking to the living God, telling him that I was a sinner but the only words I could say aloud were: "Oh God, Oh God."

I knew something revolutionary was going on inside of me. I thought, "I hope this works, because I'm making a complete fool of myself." Then the Lord brought to mind a man I had seen in Pershing Square in Los Angeles a number of years before. He was wearing a sign that said, "I'm a fool for Christ. Whose fool are you?" I thought at the time, "That's the most stupid thing I've ever seen." But as I kneeled on the floor I realized the truth of the odd sign: the cross is foolishness "to those who are perishing" (1 Corinthians 1:18). That night I knelt at the cross and believed in Jesus. I've been a fool for Christ ever since.[20]

For two thousand years, the cross of Christ has been transforming people who hated, were disobedient, rebellious and indifferent. These ones by the grace of God came to a clear understanding of how their sin had separated them from God. When we read the Epistles, we find five different meanings for sin.

First, sin means, "missing the target." In other words, we fail to be what we might have, or could have, been. All of us miss marks in our lives. Most of us do not live up to our full potential. When we realize this, we can admit to ourselves that we are sinners. Second, sin means, "a stepping across." Sin is stepping across the line, which is drawn between right and wrong. Do we always stay on the right side of the line that divides honesty from dishonesty? Do we always stay on the right side of the line when it comes to truth and lies? Do we ever, by word or by silence, twist, evade or distort the truth? Do we always stay on the right side of the line when it comes to unselfishness and courtesy as compared to selfishness and rudeness? We would be hard pressed to find anyone who doesn't step across the line. The New Testament calls that sin. Third, sin means, "a slipping across." This happens when a person momentarily loses self-control through some impulse or passion. Have we always maintained self-control? If the answer is no, then according to the New Testament, we are a sinner. A fourth definition refers to "lawlessness." It refers to a person who knows what is right, but makes a conscious choice to do the wrong thing. We know the law, but in spite of that knowledge, we will break the law. The last definition refers to a debt. It means that we fail to pay what is due—failing in duty. None of us can claim to have completely fulfilled all our duty to God or to our neighbour and therefore we are all sinners.

Forgiving another human being is a holy act, one that is required of New Testament Christians. A line of the Lord's Prayer says: *"Forgive us our trespasses, as we forgive those who trespass against us"* (Luke 11:4). We want to receive forgiveness, but many of us find it hard to forgive others. It is a New Testament principle that our reception of forgiveness is dependant upon our willingness to forgive others. Rejection, abuse or betrayal may make it hard for us to forgive others. Our natural human response to these hurtful sins is shock and confusion, especially when someone we love or respect commits them. Most people first feel hurt in their childhood and learn to develop defence mechanisms in order to protect themselves. What we don't realize is that in trying to avoid the pain and rejection, we develop an unforgiving spirit. Are the sins committed against us by others, unforgivable? According to the Scriptures, NO! It may take longer to come to a place of forgiveness for grievous sins like child abuse, rape, molestation, murder, being robbed of one's livelihood, or great betrayal. If we do not deal with the issue of forgiving those who trespass against us, we permit the perpetrators to continue to hold us in bondage. The result of that bondage is that we remain a prisoner in a cell—a cell that we build around ourselves. And the chains of unforgiveness will not allow us to leave our cells.

Furthermore, we are also called to take responsibility for the sins that we have committed against others. We cannot negate our accountability for the wrongs that we have committed. The sooner we admit to our failings, the sooner we will be set free from the prisons that hold us. If others do not have the courage or the grace to take responsibility for their sins against us, we must ask God for the grace to extend the hand of forgiveness to them. Many of us, in and outside the Church, are stuck in life because of the unforgiveness in our hearts. We carry unforgiveness against our family, our parents, living and dead, our spouses or ex-spouses, our employers, our children and even our grandchildren. Some of us are angry and bitter towards God, because God did not do what we think He should have done for us.

The Apostle Peter asked Jesus how many times we were required to forgive one another. Peter thought he was being generous when he suggested seven times. Jesus responded that we are required to forgive seventy times seven (Matthew 18:21, KJV). Jesus did not mean, however, that after four hundred and ninety times we don't have to forgive. No, in this teaching Jesus is calling us to a higher standard. He is calling us to become totally forgiving people. We need to get to the place and yes, it is hard and painful work, where we can say like Jesus on the cross, *"Father, forgive them, for they do not know what they are doing"* (Luke 23:34). When we are able to forgive like that, we set ourselves free. The person who did this evil to us, no longer controls our life. That is true liberty and we are able to achieve it, because we come to the realization that God "in Christ Jesus" has forgiven us. Therefore, we can't do any less.

We also need to learn to forgive ourselves for our failures in life. If we refuse to forgive ourselves, then who will forgive us? Forgiveness is based on the atoning work of the cross and not on anything else we do. When we sin, we withdraw our fellowship from God. It is not God who has moved, it is we who have moved. People often say, "I know that God has forgiven me and I am sure that I have forgiven those who wronged me. However, I still carry a sense of guilt and shame." This often indicates an unforgiving spirit pointed inward. It's not directed towards God or others, but at self. Until we forgive ourselves for the wrongs that we have committed, whether minor or grievous, we will not find rest in our souls.

Think about the Apostles Peter and Paul for a moment. Peter denied his Lord when it counted most. Peter would not have risen to the height that he did as an apostle if he had not forgiven himself. He knew the Lord had forgiven him, and he had the courage to look at himself again and become the man God called him to be. Paul, prior to his conversion, was bound and determined to wipe the name of Jesus off the face the earth. Where do we find the sweetest passages about forgiveness in all Scripture? Yes, in the writings of these two great men. We get some of our scriptural understanding of forgiveness from Peter's writings. We get most of our scriptural understanding from Paul's many Epistles. He would not have been able to write them, unless he was capable of forgiving himself. Many of us have been in similar places in our lives where we can't or won't forgive ourselves. We struggle with the things we have done although some of those sins may have occurred years ago. The capacity to forgive ourselves escapes us. We need to stop looking at what wretched people we are and begin to look at Jesus' cross and realize that He took every one of our sins upon Himself: "*God made him who had no sin to be sin for us, so that in him we might become the righteousness of God*" (2 Corinthians 5:21).

Paul wrote: "*Therefore, there is now no condemnation for those who are in Christ Jesus...*" (Romans 8:1). He also wrote: "*Therefore, since we have been justified through faith, we have peace with God through our Lord Jesus Christ...*" (Romans 5:1). Simply put, justification is the judicial action of God who pardons sinners and accepts them as totally cleansed or made right. Through this judicial act, God pardons and restores broken relationships with Himself. He declares that those who are justified are now righteous. How does he do this? It would seem unjust for God to declare guilty sinners suddenly righteous. According to Paul and other New Testament writers, it is a just judgment, for the basis of that righteousness is *in* Jesus Christ. Paul describes Jesus as the "last" (or second) Adam (1 Corinthians 15: 45). Jesus, acting on our behalf as the second Adam, fully obeyed the law that bound us, and on our behalf endured the retribution that should have been ours. Jesus paid the debt on our behalf. The Father doesn't overlook our lawlessness, but our lawlessness has been paid 'in' Jesus: "*For just as through the disobedience of the one man the many were made sinners, so also through the obedience of the one man the many will be made righteous*" (Romans 5:19).

For a person to realize this gift of righteousness (or right-standing with God), it must be received by faith. From the beginning of time, righteousness has always been received by faith. In Genesis, God promised Abraham and Sarah a son even though they were well past the age of producing and bearing children. Abraham believed God's promise and God declared him righteous because of his belief (Genesis 15:6). The same principle holds true in the New Testament—it is always by faith that one is declared righteous. We are declared righteous when we can look back to Calvary Hill and accept that Jesus Christ bore the punishment that was ours and died in our place. Seven hundred years before the birth of Jesus, the Prophet Isaiah described in haunting details the suffering that Jesus was to endure on our behalf:

142

He was despised and rejected by men, a man of sorrows, and familiar with suffering. Like one from whom men hide their faces he was despised, and we esteemed him not. Surely he took up our infirmities and carried our sorrows, yet we considered him stricken by God, smitten by him, and afflicted. But he was pierced for our transgressions, he was crushed for our iniquities; the punishment that brought us peace was upon him, and by his wounds we are healed. We all, like sheep, have gone astray, each of us has turned to his own way; and the LORD has laid on Him the iniquity of us all. (Isaiah 53:3-6)

God's intention through the cross was to give each one of us a fresh start and a new birth. The old spiritual says, "Were you there, when they crucified my Lord?" We may not have been physically there, but we were all mirrored there in those who crucified our Lord. On Calvary we all stood condemned. On Calvary however, Jesus took the responsibility for our sins and lawlessness upon Himself and the Father declared us justified and righteous. Yes, while we were still sinners, while we were alienated and separated from God, Jesus died for us:

But God demonstrates his own love for us in this: While we were still sinners, Christ died for us. Since we have now been justified by his blood, how much more shall we be saved from God's wrath through him! For if, when we were God's enemies, we were reconciled to him through the death of his Son, how much more, having been reconciled, shall we be saved through his life! (Romans 5:8-10)

Justification means that we have all been declared "not guilty," not on our own merits, but on the finished work of Jesus. When we accept by faith what Jesus has done for us, then we enter instantly into a new relationship with God. I hope this truth will help you understand why a dying, converted Dismas could be promised Paradise instead of eternal separation from God. The Apostle Paul sums it up, 'those who are justified will live by faith.'

DEFEAT OF DEATH

Sin was not the only thing defeated two thousand years ago on the Cross of Redemption. Death was also swallowed up in victory. The New Testament Epistles are full of Scriptures that tell us that death was defeated by the death of Jesus. Here is a sampling of that truth:

> For Christ died for sins once for all, the righteous for the unrighteous, to bring you to God. He was put to death in the body but made alive by the Spirit. (1 Peter 3:18)

> The death he died, he died to sin once for all; but the life he lives, he lives to God. (Romans 6:10)

> For this very reason, Christ died and returned to life so that he might be the Lord of both the dead and the living. (Romans 14:9)

In his great discourse on the Resurrection, Paul speaks of death losing its sting because Christ defeated death and rose victoriously:

> When the perishable has been clothed with the imperishable, and the mortal with immortality, then the saying that is written will come true: "Death has been swallowed up in victory." "Where, O death, is your victory? Where, O death, is your sting?" The sting of death is sin, and the power of sin is the law. But thanks be to God! He gives us the victory through our Lord Jesus Christ. (1 Corinthians 15:54-57)

Paul also reminds us that:

> The last enemy to be destroyed is death. (1 Corinthians 15:26)

According to John, eventually death will completely disappear:

> Then death and Hades were thrown into the lake of fire. The lake of fire is the second death. (Revelation 20:14)

From the Scriptures, we can see that our sins and the death of Jesus are linked. Paul wrote: *"the wages of sin is death"* (Romans 6:23). In other words, the ultimate penalty for sinning is death. The death of human beings however, does not appear to have been part of the plan for the world that God created. Throughout Scripture, death, both physical and spiritual, is seen, not as a natural event, but as the result of a divine judgment or a penal event. Once again, we have to look at Genesis and the fall of humanity: *"And the LORD God said, 'The man has now become like one of us, knowing good and evil. He must not be allowed to reach out his hand and take also from the tree of life and eat, and live forever.'"* (Genesis 3:22).

Is it possible that instead of either physical or spiritual death, God may have had in mind that human beings would be "translated" from this earth to the heavenly realms? There are two instances of this taking place in Scripture. The first account was in Genesis: *"Enoch walked with God; then he was no more, because God took him away"* (Genesis 5:24). The second event was recorded in 2 Kings. God had instructed Elijah to anoint and train Elisha to be a prophet for the nation of Israel. One day as Elisha and Elijah were walking along a road, Elijah was taken away: *"As they were walking along and talking together, suddenly a chariot of fire and horses of fire appeared and separated the two of them, and Elijah went up to heaven in a whirlwind"* (2 Kings 2:11).

We also find hints of translation in the New Testament. The best known verse which speaks of translation, is in Paul's letter to the Thessalonians:

> *Brothers, we do not want you to be ignorant about those who fall asleep, or to grieve like the rest of men, who have no hope. We believe that Jesus died and rose again and so we believe that God will bring with Jesus those who have fallen asleep in him. According to the Lord's own word, we tell you that we who are still alive, who are left till the coming of the Lord, will certainly not precede those who have fallen asleep. For the Lord himself will come down*

from heaven, with a loud command, with the voice of the archangel and with the trumpet call of God, and the dead in Christ will rise first. After that, we who are still alive and are left will be caught up together with them in the clouds to meet the Lord in the air. And so we will be with the Lord forever. Therefore encourage each other with these words. (1 Thessalonians 4:13-18)

Jesus also spoke of translation when He cautioned people about the end of the age and His return to this earth.

"For in the days before the flood, people were eating and drinking, marrying and giving in marriage, up to the day Noah entered the ark; and they knew nothing about what would happen until the flood came and took them all away. That is how it will be at the coming of the Son of Man. Two men will be in the field; one will be taken and the other left. Two women will be grinding with a hand mill; one will be taken and the other left. Therefore keep watch, because you do not know on what day your Lord will come."
(Matthew 24:38-42)

The New Testament gives us other hints that death is not a natural event and this is seen in Jesus' attitude to death. The Gospels record three instances where Jesus raised people from the dead. The best known is the story of Lazarus. John says that Jesus was deeply moved and troubled by Lazarus' death (John 11:33). The translations of the Greek, however, do not fully capture Jesus' reaction to the news of Lazarus' death. The Greek word translated "deeply moved" (*embrimaomai*) not only conveys strong emotions, but also conveys annoyance and displeasure. Jesus was angry that death had interrupted Lazarus' life. Jesus' vision of life saw it as a continuum, and physical death an interruption along the way.[21]

If the wages of sin is death and Jesus was sinless, would it be safe to say that He did not have to die? Could He not have been translated and escaped the cross? Both Matthew and Luke record the story of Jesus' transfiguration. This transfiguration took place shortly after

Jesus told His disciples that He had to go to Jerusalem, where He would suffer and die. After telling them this, He took Peter, James and John and went off to pray. While they were praying, Jesus was transfigured:

> *He took Peter, John and James with him and went up onto a mountain to pray. As he was praying, the appearance of his face changed, and his clothes became as bright as a flash of lightning. Two men, Moses and Elijah, appeared in glorious splendour, talking with Jesus. They spoke about his departure, which he was about to bring to fulfillment at Jerusalem.* (Luke 9:28-31)

Peter's desire was to stay on the mountain and build shelters for Moses, Elijah and Jesus. However, Jesus led the disciples down the mountain and back into the world for which He came to die. He voluntarily went to the cross of Redemption and tasted physical death for our sake. Was it a struggle for Jesus to die for us? Was He afraid of death? Some have suggested that He was, because of what took place in the Garden of Gethsemane. Let us put that event in context.

After the disciples left the Upper Room, they went to the Garden of Gethsemane, which was east of Jerusalem beyond the Kidron Valley near the Mount of Olives. It was a place of retreat for Jesus and His disciples, but this night it became a place of agony, betrayal and arrest. One could contrast Jesus' Garden of Gethsemane experience with the Garden of Eden. In the Garden of Eden, Adam succumbed to temptation and fell from grace; thus starting humanity on its downward spiral of sin and destruction. In the Garden of Gethsemane, the second Adam prevailed over temptation and re-opened the gates of grace. When Jesus arrived at the Garden, He took Peter, James and John aside and asked them to pray with Him. *"My soul is overwhelmed with sorrow to the point of death. Stay here and keep watch with me"* (Matthew 26:38). Matthew writes that Jesus then separated Himself from the apostles and fell on His face on the ground and prayed, *"Father, if you are willing, take this cup from me;*

yet not my will, but yours be done" (Luke 22:42). When He returned to the disciples, He found them sleeping. *"'Could you men not keep watch with me for one hour?' he asked Peter. 'Watch and pray so that you will not enter into temptation. The spirit is willing, but the body is weak.'"* (Matthew 26:40-41). Jesus went away a second time and prayed, *"My Father, if it is not possible for this cup to be taken away unless I drink it, may your will be done"* (Matthew 26:42).

Luke's Gospel tells us that after Jesus prayed this prayer, an angel from heaven appeared to Him and strengthened Him. The anguish in Jesus' soul must have been agonizing for Luke goes on to say, *"And being in anguish, he prayed more earnestly and his sweat was like drops of blood falling to the ground"* (Luke 22:44). The medical term for this phenomenon is "hemohidrosis" or "hematidrosis." It has been documented in patients who have experienced extreme stress or shock to their system. The capillaries around the sweat pores become fragile and leak blood into the sweat.[22] It is very difficult to imagine the kind of suffering and agony that would produce this result but it is clearly what Jesus experienced. Although Jesus was fully God, He was also fully man. He knew what lay before Him and that is why His sweat was like drops of blood falling to the ground. Was the agony that Jesus experienced a fear of death? I would respond with a resounding "no!" I don't believe that it was the fear of death that gripped Jesus in the garden. I believe it was the "cup" that Jesus would drink to the final dregs that caused such agony. From the Scriptures we can identify the various components of that cup.

The first was God's wrath, which would soon be poured out because of the sin of humanity. The prophets Isaiah and Ezekiel spoke of this cup. A cup that would bring scorn and derision, for it was a cup of sorrow, ruin and desolation. A cup that would make men stagger even though they were not drunk, and the one who drank it would be afflicted, for it is the cup of God's wrath (Isaiah 51:17 and Ezekiel 23:32-33).

The second, spoken about by John the Baptist and by the Apostle Paul, refers to the sacrificial death of Jesus. John the Baptist introduced Jesus by saying, *"Behold, the Lamb of God, who takes away the sin of the world"* (John 1:29). Paul wrote: *"Christ redeemed us from the curse of the law by becoming a curse for us, for it is written: 'Cursed is everyone who is hung on a tree'"* (Galatians. 3:13). In writing to the Corinthians, Paul puts it a different way: *"God made him who had no sin to be sin for us, so that in him we might become the righteousness of God"* (2 Corinthians 5:21).

The third component, which Jesus drank to the dregs, was the apparent abandonment by His Heavenly Father. This might have been the most bitter of this "cup" of suffering. Both Matthew and Mark tell us that on the cross, Jesus cried out, *"Eloi, Eloi, lama sabachthani"* which means *"My God, my God, why have you forsaken me?"* (Psalm 22:1 and Matthew 27:46). The debate, which has never been resolved, and has carried on through the centuries, is: Did God in fact forsake or abandon His Son on the Cross? Was Jesus Christ forsaken or did He just "feel" forsaken?

Some believe that in Jesus' death He so identified with sin that the close communion that He had always experienced with His Father was broken for the first and last time. Others say that the Father never abandoned or forsook His Son, but that His Son "felt forsaken." He "felt forsaken" in order to identify with those who have "felt forsaken" by God. As we read the stories of the saints of old in the Scriptures, I am sure that at times Abraham, Joseph, Moses, Job, David, Elijah, Jonah, Isaiah, Jeremiah, Ezekiel and even the nation of Israel "felt forsaken" by God. When they looked back on their history, however, they could clearly see that God's silence was not a sign of forsaking. Others think that the abandonment or the sense of forsakenness, which Jesus felt on the cross of Redemption, remains a mystery. I have concluded that Jesus' words; *"My God, my God, why have you forsaken me?"* need to be taken at face value.

149

The prophet Habakkuk, as we have remarked earlier, tells us that God is too pure to look upon sin and evil (Habakkuk 1:13), and so when the sin of the world was poured on God's chosen Lamb, the Father turned away. For years, I stumbled over that cry of Jesus, and drew back. Everything within me recoiled from the horror of the sin in my own heart and the sin of the world in which I lived. I was scandalized by the darkness of sin that desired to find a welcoming home in my heart. I was devastated by the truth that the crucified Jesus—whom I loved, worshipped and adored—was forsaken by the Father because of my sin. The cross, however, is there to scandalize me (us), and make me (us) stand back in awe as we hear those familiar words, *"My God, my God, why have you forsaken me?"* A very real separation occurred between the Father and the Son, because as Paul tells us, Jesus was made sin: *"God made him who had no sin to be sin for us, so that in him we might become the righteousness of God"* (2 Corinthians 5:21).

On the cross, Jesus knew the worst consequences of total identification with lost sinners. On the cross, Jesus endured separation and abandonment by His Father. It was no longer the familiar name of *"Father"* or *"Abba."* It was now, *"my God, my God."* It almost seems as if the doors of heaven had been slammed in Jesus' face. On the cross, Jesus bore all sin as if He were personally responsible for every sin committed by humanity from the beginning to the end of time. The abandonment by His heavenly Father was planned prior to the creation of the world. As someone once wrote, "The Trinity planned it, the Son endured it and the Spirit enabled Him." Paul reminds us that Jesus' work and ministry were not carried out in isolation from the Spirit or the Father: *"God was reconciling the world to himself* in Christ, *not counting men's sins against them."* (2 Corinthians 5:19, emphasis added). Jesus as the Son of God and the Son of Man, experienced everything that we as human beings experience, including death. On the cross, for our sake, the Father rejected the Son whom He loved. He did this, so that never again would another human being be absolutely forsaken. Because of God's incomprehensible love, Jesus was forsaken for us so that under no circumstances need anyone ever again be forsaken.

Let us never forget, however, that the *godforsakenness* of the cross is not the last word. The Resurrection is the last word.

CONCLUSION

In ending this section on the Cross of Redemption, I want to leave you with these truths.

First, the sins that humanity commits against God and one another are extremely horrible. What sent Jesus to the cross of Redemption was not the greed of Judas, or the envy and jealousy of the priests, or the vacillating Governor Pontius Pilate. No, the Father, out of love, permitted His Son to die for us. Jesus, as the sacrificial Lamb paid for our sins of betrayal, greed, envy, cowardice and many other sins far too numerous to mention. All of us are responsible for His death. The only way for us to be reconciled with God was for His Son to die in our place. It is not possible for us to climb up to God to be reconciled and that is why Jesus emptied Himself of all His glory and climbed down to us.

A second truth is that God's love for humanity is beyond all human comprehension. Although we don't like to think about it, God could have abandoned us to our fate. He could have left us alone to reap the fruit of our destructive behaviours. But He loves us too much. That is why He pursued us in Jesus. God loves us enough that He chose the cross as the instrument of reconciliation—a cross where He bore our judgment, condemnation, sin, guilt and death.

A third truth is that God's gift of salvation is free. Not that it did not cost God anything—in fact it cost God everything. Jesus purchased our justification, our freedom, our sanctification and our salvation by His own precious blood. There is nothing that we can pay, nor is there anything that we can add to so great a salvation.

A fourth truth is that because of the price that God has willingly paid for our salvation, His call on our lives is a call to holiness. This holy life means turning our lives to Him, repenting and turning our back on the ways of the world, the flesh and the evil one. The Gospels invite each of us to pick up our own cross and to follow the One who has gone before us.

On this third cross—the Cross of Redemption—hung Jesus of Nazareth, now acknowledged by millions as the Saviour of the world. How different from the night He was born, thirty-three years earlier. At His birth, the glory of the Lord shone around the shepherds in the field and all the angels of heaven were singing: *"Glory to God in the highest, and on earth peace to men on whom his favour rests"* (Luke 2:14). On the day of His death, the afternoon sky had turned to darkness and there was no visible sun. The sense of loneliness and despair was tangible. The voice of the crowd, crying out for blood, had by now been silenced by the darkness and the other happenings of this day. If you listened closely, in this dying hour, you would hear four distinct sounds. First, the soldiers at the foot of the cross rolling dice for the only garment Jesus owned (Psalm 22:18). The second sound came from Gestas, the crucified thief who continued to mock Jesus, *"Aren't you the Christ?"* Third, Dismas' words, *"Jesus, Remember Me…"* echoed in the air. Finally, the last sound you would hear was sobbing, from those standing near the cross. One of them was His mother, Mary. Simeon's words had come to pass, *"And a sword will pierce your own soul too"* (Luke 2:35). On this day, you could not hear the flutter of angel wings, for all of heaven remained silent.

On this third cross, was a dying Saviour. On this cross of Redemption, Jesus fully embraced the sin of the first man, Adam, to the sin of the last person who will be born into this world. All of it, along with death, has been poured out on this Cross. Jesus drank the cup to the very dregs. Indeed, *"It is finished!"* (John 19:30).

CHAPTER 5

EVIDENCE OF
THE RESURRECTION

On the first day of the week, very early in the morning, the women took the spices they had prepared and went to the tomb. They found the stone rolled away from the tomb, but when they entered, they did not find the body of the Lord Jesus. While they were wondering about this, suddenly two men in clothes that gleamed like lightning stood beside them. In their fright the women bowed down with their faces to the ground, but the men said to them, "Why do you look for the living among the dead? He is not here; he has risen!" (Luke 24:1-6)

For the past almost two thousand years the Church of Christ has said or sung the following canticle:

Alleluia! Christ our Passover has been sacrificed for us;
therefore let us keep the feast,
Not with the old leaven, the leaven of malice and evil,
but with the unleavened bread of sincerity and truth. Alleluia!

Christ being raised from the dead will never die again;
death no longer has dominion over him.
The death that he died, he died to sin, once for all;
but the life he lives, he lives to God.
So also consider yourselves dead to sin,
and alive to God in Jesus Christ our Lord. Alleluia!

Christ has been raised from the dead,
the first fruits of those who have fallen asleep.
For since by a man came death,
by a man has come also the resurrection of the dead.
For as in Adam all die,
so also in Christ shall all be made alive. Alleluia!
(1 Corinthians 5:7-8; Romans 6:9-11; 1 Corinthians 15:
20-22)

This canticle is a blend of Scriptures from Paul's letters to the churches in Rome and Corinth, Scriptures that are the foundation stone of the Christian faith. It reminds us that we have been redeemed by the perfect sacrifice, and urges us to keep this feast in sincerity and truth. As the Israelites were instructed to keep the Passover, we must continue to celebrate the Resurrection. The canticle also reminds us that Jesus will never die again; and it reminds us that, as believers, we were made dead to sin and death, and alive to God, in Christ Jesus our Lord.

There are some aspects of the Christian faith that are negotiable. Some doctrines differ from denomination to denomination. The one absolute to the orthodox Christian faith however, is Jesus' physical resurrection from the dead. I don't think one can write a book about the cross, and not deal with what came after the crucifixion—the physical resurrection of Jesus. In this chapter I present the biblical evidence of Jesus' resurrection. We must decide whether or not that evidence is credible and whether or not it is reasonable to believe that such a miracle took place over two thousand years ago.

Two of my younger brothers are police officers in Ontario. Their service records indicate that they are very competent and responsible officers. They know that in order to send those who break the law to prison, there must be evidence that the laws of the land have been broken. Suspicion or even certainty in their minds is not enough. They must be able to present that evidence in a clear way to the courts. They must also be careful in collecting that evidence, as defence lawyers and the courts will subject it to close examination. When the evidence is finally presented, it is up to a judge or a jury to determine the guilt or innocence of the accused. Under the law, the judge or jury may decide the guilt or innocence of an individual only on the strength of the evidence presented to them. When Jesus physically rose from the dead, He broke the laws of nature. Is there enough evidence to support this event? Is it reasonable to believe that it happened?

The writers of the New Testament did not attempt to prove the resurrection. They recorded that the resurrection took place and they included the many stories of resurrection appearances. They did not need to prove the resurrection beyond any reasonable doubt. God's words to Israel delivered by his servant Moses are recorded in Deuteronomy: "*On the testimony of two or three witnesses a man shall be put to death, but no one shall be put to death on the testimony of only one witness*" (Deuteronomy 17:6). In other words, the evidence to an event that was attested to by two or more witnesses was to be accepted as legally conclusive. This was the case with Jesus' resurrection appearances. From the two angels at the empty tomb; through the group of women who went to the tomb on Sunday morning; through Peter and John who ran to the tomb; and to the gathering of the apostles—in each of these incidences there were two or more witnesses. I must point out, however, that the Gospels do record two single appearances by the Risen Christ. One was to Mary Magdalene on Sunday morning and the second was to the Apostle Paul on the road to Damascus. Thus the testimonies of His resurrection are overwhelming and there is no question that they met all the legal requirements of the day.

Two thousand years later, however, to prove the resurrection beyond all shadow of doubt without accepting this evidence, is like trying to prove the existence of God. From Genesis to Revelation, the writers never attempt to prove the existence of God. God cannot be proved. God can only be believed and encountered. It is when we begin to believe that the revelation of the existence of God becomes clear. The God of the Bible is not the "First Cause" or the "Unmoved Mover" as suggested in some philosophical arguments; the Bible says that He is a living God who made humanity. Scripture never argues about God's existence, it always assumes God as the basis for all else. When the disciples began to preach the resurrection, they simply told people what had happened. I will present here, the evidence of the resurrection, so that you can draw your own conclusions as to whether it was an authentic event.

I must share with you first what, according to the writers of the New Testament, happened two thousand years ago. Two resurrection appearances are recorded in Matthew's Gospel. The first took place on Easter morning when the two Marys went to the tomb to anoint Jesus' body. When they arrived at the tomb, angels met them and told them that Jesus had risen. They instructed the two women to go and tell the rest of the disciples that Jesus had risen and would meet them in Galilee (Matthew 28:1-10). According to Matthew, it was in Galilee that the second resurrection appearance took place. It happened on a mountain, which Jesus had told the disciples to go to. Jesus appeared to them there and gave them the Great Commission to go into the world and preach the Gospel:

> Then Jesus came to them and said, "All authority in heaven and on earth has been given to me. Therefore go and make disciples of all nations, baptizing them in the name of the Father and of the Son

and of the Holy Spirit, and teaching them to obey everything I have commanded you. And surely I am with you always, to the very end of the age." (Matthew 28:18-20)

Mark's Gospel tells a slightly different story. Mark says on that first Sunday, three women went to the tomb, Mary Magdalene, Mary the mother of James, and Salome (Mark 16:1-8). At the tomb they encountered an angel who told them that Jesus had risen and they should go and tell the disciples this good news. But according to Mark they didn't do that. We read instead: "*Trembling and bewildered, the women went out and fled from the tomb. They said nothing to anyone because they were afraid*" (Mark 16:8). This is where the Gospel of Mark ends, according to the earliest manuscripts. Although there are twelve additional verses at the end of this chapter, scholars are not sure if they were originally part of Mark's gospel, and so I will not present any evidence from those verses.

When we turn to Luke's Gospel, we find that Luke records three resurrection appearances. Angels outside the tomb told a number of women that Jesus had been raised and the tomb was empty. Luke didn't identify the women, but most scholars conclude that they were probably the three that were mentioned in Matthew's Gospel. The message they carried from the two angels back to the other disciples is what matters.

> *"Why do you look for the living among the dead? He is not here; he has risen! Remember how he told you, while he was still with you in Galilee: 'The Son of Man must be delivered into the hands of sinful men, be crucified and on the third day be raised again.'"* (Luke 24:5b-7)

The second resurrection appearance recorded in Luke's Gospel is the story of two disciples on the road to Emmaus (Luke 24:13-35). For twenty-two verses the historian Luke records in great detail the story of the two disciples who were making their way home the Sunday after the crucifixion. In this account we realize that these two had heard about the resurrection, but did not believe the rumours that were floating around. Jesus appeared and walked with these two for several miles, reviewing the Scriptures, which spoke of the death and resurrection of the Christ. It was not until Jesus broke bread with them at the evening meal that they recognized the risen Jesus: *"When he was at the table with them, he took bread, gave thanks, broke it and began to give it to them. Then their eyes were opened and they recognized him, and he disappeared from their sight"* (Luke 24:30). Once these disciples recognized Jesus, they hurried back to Jerusalem to tell the rest of the disciples that they were first hand witnesses to the resurrection.

Where did they find the disciples? Scholars believe that the disciples were now reassembled in the Upper Room. The risen Jesus made His third appearance here. The disciples thought that He was a ghost and to prove that He was not, He ate a piece of fish. Ghosts do not consume food, nor do they have nail pierced hands and feet. They recognized that it was Jesus, but Jesus' body was not the body that He had died with. This is part of the mystery of death and resurrection. Scripture says that the bodies in which we live cannot inherit the kingdom of God because they are vessels tainted by sin. Since sin cannot enter into the presence of God, our earthly bodies, as we know them, will not enter God's holy presence. Jesus, as the *"first-fruit"* from the dead, now had a new and glorified body as His first body contained the sin and death of the world, which He had assumed for us on the cross (1 Corinthians 15:20).

People have always been curious and anxious to know what our new glorified bodies will look like in heaven. Paul addressed this question in his letter to the Church in Corinth. Paul wrote:

> *There are also heavenly bodies and there are earthly bodies...the body that is sown is perishable, it is raised imperishable; it is sown in dishonour, it is raised in glory; it is sown in weakness, it is raised in power; it is sown a natural body, it is raised a spiritual body...Listen, I tell you a mystery: We will not all sleep, but we*

will all be changed—in a flash, in the twinkling of an eye, at the last trumpet. For the trumpet will sound, the dead will be raised imperishable, and we will be changed. (1 Corinthians 15:40, 42-44; 51-52)

People also want to know if we will recognize each other in heaven? I have no doubt that we will. When the disciples initially encountered Jesus after the resurrection, they had difficulty recognizing Him. Why? Not only because His resurrection was so unexpected, but His physical body, was changed to a glorified spiritual body. A body that could now travel to many places without restriction, and walk into rooms notwithstanding locked doors. As Paul says, the resurrected body is a mystery and cannot be fully understood on this side of the veil. I think we are not meant to fully understand.

When we turn to John's Gospel, John has recorded four resurrection appearances. The first one is private, between Jesus and Mary Magdalene. I believe that Mary Magdalene had a very special place in the heart of Jesus and He appeared to her because she needed that revelation. Mary's hope was Jesus. He had changed her life and she had followed Him ever since. She was the one out of whom Jesus had cast seven demons, freeing her from untold torment (Luke 8:2). Jesus had given her a reason to live and had restored her worth and dignity as a child of God. Mary was one of the few disciples at the foot of the cross the day Jesus died (Matthew 27:56). Love brought Mary to the foot of the cross and love brought her to the garden that first Easter Sunday. On Resurrection Sunday, Jesus could have paraded through the streets of Jerusalem. He could have knocked on Pilate's front door. He could have confronted the High Priest and the Pharisees who had condemned Him to death. But the first person the resurrected Lord showed Himself to was a woman who needed hope. *"Woman, why are you crying? Who is it you are looking for?"* (John 20:15). Then Jesus said very tenderly, *"Mary,"* and she recognized His voice (John 20:16). Can you imagine the day when you get to heaven and Jesus speaks your name? What a glorious celebration that will be!

The second resurrection appearance recorded by John, took place in the upper room where, he tells us, the doors were locked and bolted. Jesus in His new body came and stood in the midst of them and said those familiar words, *"Peace be with you!"* John also records that it was at this time that Jesus gave to the disciples the same authority that He had to forgive sins. *"If you forgive anyone their sins, they are forgiven"* (John 20:23).

When Jesus went to the upper room that day, the Apostle Thomas was absent. When the disciples told him about Jesus' appearance, he refused to believe what they said about the resurrection. A week later however, with Thomas present, Jesus made His third resurrection appearance and chided Thomas for his doubt. From that day forward, Thomas became known as "doubting Thomas," not so much because of his doubt, but because of his spirit of unbelief. He refused to believe the evidence presented to him by the other disciples. No, he said, he had to see and feel personally the nail-pierced hands, and put his own hand into Jesus' side, before he would be willing to believe (John 20:25). What Jesus said to Thomas is really the tenth Beatitude we find in the Gospels and we are the benefactors of a wonderful promise, *"Thomas, because you have seen me, you have believed: blessed are those who have not seen and yet have believed"* (John 20:29). Thomas wanted practical proof. He wanted to see and feel the scars of the crucifixion. He needed to physically "touch" this risen Jesus before he could accept the resurrection as true. Practical people have a difficult time with the news of the resurrection. If you knew that someone had died last Friday, and you were now being told that the deceased was alive, you would say it was outside the realm of practical possibility. Dead people do not come back to life. Roman soldiers did not make mistakes when they put a man to death by crucifixion. Thomas' response to the news of the resurrection is easy to understand and is not that different from the response of others who had heard the news.

The fourth appearance of the risen Jesus related in John's Gospel is to seven disciples at the Sea of Galilee. I wonder if John included this story for Peter's sake? It was at this time that Peter was reinstated as the leader of the disciples. All four Gospels tell the story of Peter's betrayal of Jesus, but John's is the only Gospel that tells of his reinstatement. That morning Jesus came to Peter as a friend, a friend who prayed for Peter when he was weak, and forgave when he failed. Jesus was a friend who loved Peter and came to heal a painful memory. Jesus was a friend who believed in Peter and laid down His life so that His friend could have eternal life.

In the Book of Acts, there are three recorded resurrection appearances, but there may well have been more. Luke wrote the Book of Acts and he says: *"Jesus showed himself to these men and gave many convincing proofs that he was alive. He appeared to them over a period of forty days"* (Acts 1:3). How many times He appeared, is not known for sure, but we do know that it was on numerous occasions. The second recorded resurrection appearance took place on Ascension Day, the day Jesus ascended into the heavens. We do not know how many people were there when Jesus ascended, but in his letter to the Church in Corinth, Paul tells of a time when Jesus appeared to five hundred all at once. The Ascension may have been that occasion, but scholars are not sure (Acts 1:9). The third resurrection appearance took place when Jesus appeared to the murderous Saul who became the converted Paul on the road to Damascus, as described in Acts Chapter nine.

Paul's letter to the Church in Corinth tells of four different appearances of the risen Jesus:

> ... *that he was raised on the third day according to the Scriptures, and that he appeared to Peter, and then to the Twelve. After that, he appeared to more than five hundred of the brothers at the same time, most of whom are still living, though some have fallen asleep. Then he appeared to James, then to all the apostles, and last of all he appeared to me also...* (1 Corinthians 15:4b-8)

All told, in these five books of the Bible we have on record eleven to fourteen different resurrection appearances. What do we do with them?

HALLUCINATION

It has been suggested that in their grief, the disciples hallucinated Jesus' resurrection. If that is true, then it is not just the doctrine of the resurrection that collapses, but the whole of Christianity. No explanation of the resurrection appearances is without difficulty. The *Victoria Times Colonist* daily newspaper reported part of a written interview with Professor Ben Witherington III, who teaches at Kentucky's Asbury Theological Seminary. Witherington wrote: "Whether we are comfortable with it or not, Christianity does indeed stand or fall on certain historical facts, not historical claims. The Christian faith is not mere faith in faith—ours or someone else's—but rather a belief about the significance of certain historical events."[1] Witherington asserts that we cannot evade the basic questions: Are the claims of the resurrection true or not? How do we assess the trustworthiness of the witness? Witherington gives us three options: Something extraordinary happened, but the disciples misunderstood it, or, nothing happened, but the disciples mistakenly thought it did, or, Jesus did rise bodily from the grave and appeared to people who correctly understood what had happened. Witherington insists that in Jesus' time, resurrection was materialistic. The witnesses knew that something had happened to Jesus' body after death, and it wasn't just their wishful thinking. Witherington reads all four Gospels as stressing the material nature of Jesus' resurrected body. He suggests that no mere vision or spiritual experience would have changed the disheartened disciples. "Only an encounter with the Risen Lord would do that," he says. Nor does Witherington find hallucination plausible. Early testimony passed on to Paul says that Jesus appeared at different times to different people and groups of people. Witherington says that there is no such thing as "contagious hallucination." He thinks it unlikely that Gospel writers in a male dominated society would have invented Jesus' first appearances which were to women. Witherington concludes the best explanation is that the first Christians were utterly convinced that something marvellous happened to Jesus' body, and they were "in personal and visible contact" with the Risen Lord on that first Easter.

THIEVERY

From the moment that Jesus rose from the dead, people have been trying to refute it. Every generation of the church has fought to maintain the truth of the resurrection. Our present generation is beset by those who question the divinity of Jesus and the literal reality of His physical resurrection on Easter Sunday. If you remove the death, burial and resurrection of Jesus, what is left of the Christian faith? Today there is a growing tendency to take what I would call "a salad bar" approach to theology and to the Scriptures. Using this method, the Scriptures are used to justify personal prejudices, or to strip the Gospel of its life-saving power. Wrong teaching will create the idea that the Scriptures are filled with textual errors or are simply a collection of myths—including the physical resurrection of Jesus Christ from the dead.

The lies about the resurrection began on the morning of the resurrection. The soldiers guarding the tomb reported to the Chief Priests what had occurred in the garden. This was exactly what the Chief Priests were afraid of. They admitted that they were afraid that the disciples would steal the body. What they didn't admit, I think, was their anxiety that Jesus was all He said He was and that there would be a resurrection. After all, the resurrection had been prophesied in the Old Testament and the Priests knew the Scriptures. They had asked Pilate to place a guard and a seal on the grave. The Scripture tells of it thus:

The chief priests and the Pharisees went to Pilate. "Sir," they said, "We remember that while he was still alive that deceiver said, 'After three days, I will rise again'. So give the order for the tomb to be made secure until the third day. Otherwise, his disciples may come and steal the body and tell the people that he has been raised from the dead. This last deception will be worse than the first." "Take a guard," Pilate answered. "Go, make the tomb as secure as you know how." So they went and made the tomb secure by putting a seal on the stone and posting the guard. (Matthew 27:62-65)

What is surprising is that nowhere in the history of the early Church is it recorded that anyone ever came out and accused the disciples of stealing Jesus' body. On many occasions they were brought to trial for their belief in the resurrection and their preaching in the Name of Jesus, but they were not ever accused publicly of stealing the body.

"There was a violent earthquake, for an angel of the Lord came down from heaven and, going to the tomb, rolled back the stone and sat on it ... The guards were so afraid of him that they shook and became like dead men" (Matthew 28:2-4). When the guards reported to the Chief Priests, they devised a plan: *"...they gave the soldiers a large sum of money, telling them, 'You are to say, "His disciples came during the night and stole him away while we were asleep."'... So the soldiers took the money and did as they were instructed"* (Matthew 28:12-15). The soldiers were paid to lie about what had happened. Why would they lie? A large sum of money will certainly help some look the other way. There could also be another reason. If you were one of the soldiers sent to guard the tomb and the "dead" man you were guarding disappeared, what other duty would you then be fit for? The soldiers guarding the tomb must have thought that Pilate had lost his mind, instructing them to guard the tomb of a man who, beyond any shadow of doubt, was dead. How could they go back to their commanding officer and tell him that the man who was dead and buried had risen from the grave? How could they tell him that they had seen an angel break Pilate's seal and roll back the stone? The

easy thing to do was take the money and run. I am willing to wager though, that these men were haunted by that event for the rest of their lives.

It is interesting to note the means that the Jewish authorities used in their desperate attempts to eliminate Jesus as the Messiah. They used treason to have Him betrayed. They broke their own laws in trying Him. They used slander to charge Him to Pilate. And then they used bribery to try to silence the truth about Him. They failed. Great is the truth, and it will prevail. It is a fact that all of humanity's evil manipulations cannot in the end stop the truth. The Gospel of goodness is greater than plots of wickedness.

WHY BELIEVE?

The Christian faith is planted firmly upon the belief in the physical resurrection of Jesus from the dead. If there had been only one or two appearances to individual disciples after His resurrection, we could dismiss it. Over a forty day period, however, Jesus' risen appearances were to individuals, to groups, in the country, in the upper room, by a lake, on the road, and in about every setting that one can imagine. Certain people may be subject to hallucinations, but it would take an awful lot to convince people like Peter, Thomas and Paul. These men's lives were changed forever.

According to tradition, Thomas went on to become a missionary in India and was martyred there.[2] In proclaiming the resurrection, Peter had everything to lose, but he did not waver. He stood in front of high priests, magistrates and those in authority, and not once did he back down. Fifty days after the resurrection, Peter boldly preached the news of the risen Jesus to a crowd of three thousand. Peter too was crucified for his faith. According to tradition, when they came to crucify him, he insisted on being crucified upside down, as he felt that he was not worthy to die in the same way his Master had died.[3]

Paul can be described as the greatest missionary who ever lived. Prior to his encounter with Jesus on the road to Damascus, he was

Saul the persecutor, whose sole purpose in life was to wipe out the name of Jesus of Nazareth and destroy His followers. But God intervened in his life and, like Dismas, he was changed in an instant: *"'Saul, Saul, why do you persecute me?' 'Who are you, Lord?' 'I am Jesus, whom you are persecuting'"* (Acts 9:4-5). Saul is mentioned a number of times in Scripture prior to this conversion story. He was present and gave his approval as a mob stoned Stephen to death. Stephen's crime was preaching about Jesus' resurrection. After Stephen's martyrdom, Saul deliberately set out to destroy the Church. The historian Luke begins chapter 9 of Acts with these words: *"Saul was still breathing out murderous threats against the Lord's disciples"* (Acts 9:1). His desire was to contain Jesus' followers in Jerusalem, but some of them escaped to Damascus. Saul then gained the approval of the High Priest to go to Damascus and arrest all those who belonged to this sect. In a modern context one may see Saul as fanatical as a modern terrorist in his desire to eliminate Jesus' followers—an ancestor of those who gird themselves with explosives and set out to destroy their enemies. He was no longer content to guard the cloaks of those who threw the stones, he wanted stones in his own hands; he wanted blood on his hands.[4]

In Paul's later writings, he makes it very clear that it was only by the grace of God that he was converted and called to be an apostle to the Gentiles. It is interesting to note the words that Paul uses to describe his conversion experience. Again and again in his writings he said that he went to arrest and seize those who were following Jesus. Instead, Paul says, God "arrested" and "seized hold of him." He suffered greatly for the kingdom of God. He described some of the suffering he endured in his second letter to the Church in Corinth:

> *Are they servants of Christ? (I am out of my mind to talk like this.) I am more. I have worked much harder, been in prison more frequently, been flogged more severely, and been exposed to death again and again. Five times I received from the Jews the forty lashes minus one. Three times I was beaten with rods, once I was*

*stoned, three times I was shipwrecked, I spent a night and a day
in the open sea. I have been constantly on the move. I have been
in danger from rivers, in danger from bandits, in danger from my
own countrymen, in danger from Gentiles; in danger in the city, in
danger in the country, in danger at sea, and in danger from false
brothers. I have laboured and toiled and often gone without sleep;
I have known hunger and thirst and have often gone without food;
I have been cold and naked. Besides everything else, I face daily the
pressure of my concern for all the churches. Who is weak, and I do
not feel weak? Who is led into sin, and I do not inwardly burn?*
(2 Corinthians 11:22-29)

Why did Paul suffer so much? He suffered because of his belief in
and teaching about the resurrection. Preaching of the resurrection
eventually cost Paul his life and he was beheaded.[5] These three men
were pillars of the New Testament Church. The price that these
witnesses were willing to pay should encourage us to place our hope
and belief in the teaching they have left behind.

When we examine all the evidence that is available about the
Easter-faith, we have to reject it or accept it. If you reject the
resurrection, however, you must also reject Jesus. Why? Because
again and again throughout His ministry, He prophesied that He
would suffer, die and rise again. If you dismiss His claims about the
resurrection, then you must dismiss His teaching and example, His
sacrifice, and His claim to have destroyed sin and death. Everything
about Jesus hinges upon His resurrection from the dead. Dismiss it
and you dismiss Jesus.

Sadly, many so-called theologians and scholars of today have
dismissed the physical resurrection of Jesus and replaced it with a
spiritual resurrection. Some of these scholars will admit that Jesus'
resurrection from the grave is Christianity's central belief, but to
many of them, the telling thing isn't what was claimed, but who
made the claim—namely, Jesus' followers. These scholars teach that
after Jesus died, somewhere and somehow these disciples found the

courage to proclaim the meaning of His life. That turnaround is what they claim is meant by the resurrection. Their understanding of Jesus' resurrection is that it is to be viewed only as a symbol or sign of the human possibility of transformation, either personal or social. I would describe this kind of thinking as disbelief, which is the unwillingness or inability to believe.

Traditionally the Apostle Thomas has been described as a "doubter." Healthy doubt is not a bad thing. When Jesus finally appeared to Thomas, He didn't really rebuke him for doubting, but instead invited him to move beyond doubt into faith. Genuine doubt can be the path that God will use to bring us to Himself. We can hide behind our doubts of course, and never commit ourselves to belief. People who claim that they do not know "if God exists" are called agnostics. If you seriously wish to discover the truth about the existence of God, you will find that you cannot remain an agnostic. You have to decide one way or the other. It has been written, "It's not that Christianity has been tried and found wanting; rather, it has not been tried." I don't believe for a moment that God objects to genuine doubt. Genuine doubters are in reality, genuine seekers. God honours seekers by revealing Himself to them: *"You will seek me and find me when you seek me with all your heart. I will be found by you,' declares the LORD..."* (Jeremiah 29:13-14). God may not reveal Himself to us in a physical form, but He reaches down into our hearts and reveals Himself to be real and alive.

Many years ago after an encounter with the living God, it was my decision to believe the biblical record that God raised Jesus from the dead. I based my conclusions on the empty tomb, the numerous resurrection appearances and the beginning of the Christian Church. I based it on the conversion of so many down through the years. I based it on the centrality of the resurrection in the Church's teaching and preaching. I am firmly convinced that, "On the third day, He rose again in accordance with the Scriptures, He ascended into heaven and is seated at the right hand of the Father" (*Nicene Creed*).[6]

Over the years, I have become as convinced as was Paul, that if Jesus has not been raised, then our faith is futile and we are to be pitied more than anyone else (1 Corinthians 15:19).

I accept the resurrection of Jesus not as an invention or hallucination of the community of disciples, but as an historical event. Nor do I believe that the disciples stole Jesus' body. Instead, my confession of faith includes the words, *"Christ has died, Christ is risen and Christ will come again."* I do not believe that the evidence warrants any other conclusion. Will you also believe with me?

CHAPTER 6

WHICH CROSS WILL YOU CHOOSE?

See to it that you do not refuse him who speaks. If they did not escape when they refused him who warned them on earth, how much less will we, if we turn away from him who warns us from heaven? (Hebrews 12:25)

Three crosses on a lonely hill,
A thief on either side
And, in between, the Son of God
How wide the gulf—how wide!

Yet one thief spanned it with the words
"Oh Lord, remember me":
The other scoffed and turned aside
To lost eternity.

Forsaken is the hilltop now
And all the crosses gone

170

But in believing hearts of men
The centre cross lives on

And still, as when these sentinels
First met earth's wondering view
The presence of the Lord divides-
Upon which side are you?[1]

We are nearing the end of our journey. We have examined in depth the stories behind the three crosses on that lonely hill outside the city of Jerusalem. Two of the three men crucified were found guilty and sentenced according to the laws of the day. One was found innocent but received the same sentence, death by crucifixion.

On the *Cross of Redemption,* hung the Son of Man. We have seen that He was there, not by accident, but by choice. His purpose in coming into this world was to offer Himself as a living sacrifice. He offered Himself so that the sin and death of humanity would be swallowed up and defeated in His death. Jesus took upon Himself the punishment that was ours. Clear evidence has been presented that Jesus suffered and died on this cross so that we could have life. We know that death did not have the final word, for three days later He rose from the dead.

The reality is that we are not forced to accept this great sacrifice. Every person made in the image of God has a free choice and that right to choose will never be violated. This truth is evident all through the Gospels. Throughout Jesus' ministry, there were some who came and said that they wanted to follow Him. When Jesus told them the true cost of discipleship, however, they turned away. They were not willing to offer what it would take. You will never find a place in the Gospels, where, in spite of these constant rejections, Jesus ever compromised His message of what it meant to be His disciple. In spite of His primary desire to restore people to God, Jesus refused to force anyone to accept Him. As it was true two thousand years ago, it is true today.

In my church office hangs a copy of a well-known painting by Holman Hunt.[2] The original hangs in Keble College Chapel, Oxford, England. The painting is entitled, "The Light of the World." Jesus is depicted standing at a garden door. The door is ivy-covered, as if long closed. In Jesus' left hand is a lantern, representing the lamp of truth. With His right hand He knocks gently on the door. His eyes are filled with compassion and His expression can best be described as one of yearning. The surprising thing about the door is that there is no handle or latch on its outside. Jesus cannot open the door from His side. Hunt's intention in this picture was to remind us that God does not force His way into our lives. He also conveys the quiet message that Jesus comes to the door of your heart and knocks. While He stands there, your life goes on, but He patiently waits and knocks. You must open the door yourself, for the only latch or handle is on the inside. The Scripture that supports the concept of this painting is Revelation 3:20, *"Here I am! I stand at the door and knock. If anyone hears my voice and opens the door, I will come in and eat with him, and he with me."* Jesus invites us to be in relationship with Him. This relationship is based on the personal invitation that we are called to extend to Jesus. If we extend the invitation, He has promised to come into our lives. He will forgive our sins and cleanse us from all unrighteousness. He will remove from us the sting and the fear of death. We can be assured that we will not be alone on the day we die: *"Yea, though I walk through the valley of the shadow of death, I will fear no evil: for thou art with me; thy rod and thy staff they comfort me...and I will dwell in the house of the LORD forever"* (Psalm 23: 4 & 6b, KJV).

When Jesus comes into our lives, His intention is to develop us into the holy people of God. Over time we will learn to yield ourselves to Him. The Holy Spirit will direct our personal interests and we will learn to walk in harmony with God's plan for our lives.

We will learn to embrace the things of God and we will grow in our love for Him and for others. As we walk in step with God's Spirit, we will be able to put aside the attractions of the world, the flesh and the evil one. No longer will we look at the cross as an object of shame, humiliation and darkness. We will see it as a symbol of victory—a sign that our sin and death are overcome. Within us will beat a heart that is in communion with God, who loves us so tenderly that our lives cannot help but be filled with the love of Jesus. We will become all that God intended us to be.

> *"For I know the plans I have for you," declares the LORD, "plans to prosper you and not to harm you, plans to give you hope and a future. Then you will call upon me and come and pray to me, and I will listen to you. You will seek me and find me when you seek me with all your heart. I will be found by you," declares the LORD.* (Jeremiah 29:11-14)

On the *Cross of Rejection* hung Gestas. From his cross, Gestas refused to reach out and accept that Jesus, who was dying on the cross next to him, was the Saviour of the world. His heart was closed to the possibility of a future life in the kingdom of God. His focus in life was on self. He was lost, but did not realize the depth of his lostness. Many people in this world are in that condition. They do not know or love God. They will not say that they hate God; they are just indifferent to Him. Their philosophy in life is to "eat, drink and be merry, for tomorrow we may die." Or if they are not pursuing temporal pleasures, they are caught up in pursuing other fleeting goals. Goals they think will quench the deep thirst and hunger in their souls. We must, however, heed the warnings of the Gospel:

> *Then he (Jesus) called the crowd to him along with his disciples and said: "If anyone would come after me, he must deny himself and take up his cross and follow me. For whoever wants to save his life will lose it, but whoever loses his life for me and for the gospel will save it. What good is it for a man to gain the whole world, yet*

forfeit his soul? Or what can a man give in exchange for his soul?"
(Mark 8:34-37)

It is disheartening to see that the only goals in life for so many are the temporal treasures that this world can offer. What they do not realize is that they have already passed from life to death, for they are spiritually dead. They have fallen into a familiar trap:

> *The god of this age has blinded the minds of unbelievers, so that they cannot see the light of the gospel of the glory of Christ, who is the image of God.* (2 Corinthians 4:4)

Let me be very clear that in our pursuit of God, we must realize that He is not looking for "religious" people. He is looking for people who desire to be in genuine relationship with Him. Jesus' greatest enemies were the supposed religious leaders of Israel. As you read through the Gospels though, these are the only individuals that Jesus ever chastised. They were full of self-righteousness and purported to be safeguarding the nation, by arranging for the crucifixion of God's only Son. God seeks those who will follow Him honestly and sincerely.

Gestas was within an arm's reach of the Saviour, but he spent his time railing against Him. There is no question that he wanted deliverance, but it was deliverance from his cross and death. Now some may think that there is no rush to make ourselves right with God. After all, didn't God save Dismas at the last possible moment? That is true, but that particular Gospel story speaks of God's outstanding grace in action. We have no right to assume that God's loving grace provides us licence to continue living a life of sin and self-indulgence. Nor should anyone take the risk of presuming on the grace of God. I have sat at the bedside of many who were facing death. Very rarely have they focused on the things of God. Most often they struggle with the pain of dying and the uncertainty of what lies ahead. For some, their hearts have grown hard and they cannot hear in their dying hours God's message of love and mercy. As he was dying, Dismas appealed to Gestas, but Gestas shut his ears to his voice. The writer of the Epistle to the Hebrews, urges us that if we hear the voice of God, we should not harden our hearts against Him:

> *See to it, brothers, that none of you has a sinful, unbelieving heart that turns away from the living God. But encourage one another daily, as long as it is called Today, so that none of you may be hardened by sin's deceitfulness…as has just been said: "Today, if you hear his voice, do not harden your hearts…"* (Hebrews 3:12-15)

Every human being's eternal destination is determined by his or her response to God. Please God, let it be a favourable response.

That is the prayer of my heart for each of you reading this book. God yearns to be in relationship with you. You are His beloved child and He proved it by sending His Son to die for you. God's desire is that not one of His children should be shut out of His kingdom. He is more than willing to remove the blinders from our eyes and be found. As a pastor, I have discovered that we can't leave the matters of the soul to the very end—that may be too late. I implore you on Jesus' behalf, do not forsake or turn away from this great salvation.

On the *Cross of Reception*, Dismas was changed from a dying sinner to a dying saint. Dismas' story is all about grace. In fact, the Gospel story is all about grace. Grace reaching out; grace embracing; grace accepting and grace changing sinners into saints. No person is ever beyond the reach of God's mercy and grace, or disqualified from receiving God's kindness, except by their own will. If all we do is ask Jesus to "remember us," then that is what He will do.

I love this story in the Gospel of Luke, for I have no difficulty in relating to Dismas. He and I have a lot in common, for in the blink of an eye, God changed my life. Every child of God has a story to tell, and this is mine. My first encounter with God took place in a church in Ottawa, Ontario in May 1979. This marked the beginning of a journey with God that helped shape my love for the cross and for my Lord Jesus Christ. In May of 1979, I was at my wit's end. I had suffered through a personal tragedy. I had been betrayed badly, and I saw no purpose in carrying on with this mystery called life. I was depressed and very angry and I took that anger out on God. I blamed him for my life and I was bound and determined to hold Him accountable for the mess that I was in. There is no point in being angry with God, unless you tell Him. I knew that I needed to go back to the church that I had discarded earlier in life to make sure that God received the message first hand.

I spent months wandering in and out of churches. As I knelt in the pews and looked up at crucifix after crucifix I told God how angry and hurt I was, and asked Him what He was going to do about it. My words of anger and hostility were met with an impassive silence. I was almost ready to give up in despair of getting an answer, when a friend invited me to a church to hear a football player talk about the Christian faith. That church service was unlike anything I had ever experienced. When I walked in, I found joyful people who genuinely seemed to like and love each other. They appeared to have an authentic relationship with the God they were worshiping. It was as though I was in another world. My previous experience of church was that it was boring and staid. That night I found myself listening to a man talk about Jesus as if he knew Him personally. I didn't think it was possible for anyone to *know* Jesus, but this man talked and spoke as if Jesus was his best friend. Although the church was full, I felt as though the speaker and I were the only ones there. His words cut like a sword into my heart. When his talk was over, he invited those in the audience who wanted to know Jesus and to invite Him into their lives, to put up their hands. I was a skeptic, my heart was hard and I was still so very angry with God. But I had nothing to lose. I had tried everything else to bring rest to my soul. Nothing had worked. I didn't know it at the time, but grace was at work in me. With my head bowed, my eyes closed and my heart thumping a thousand miles an hour, I mustered up the courage to say *"Yes,"* to Jesus, *"Come into this heart of stone."*

WHICH CROSS WILL YOU CHOOSE?

I don't know what I expected, but what happened to me can only be described as life changing. The service leader asked for a show of hands of those who had accepted Jesus. With fear and trembling, I put my hand up. Suddenly I was bathed in what I can only describe as a shower of love. It was as though I was no longer sitting in a pew, but instead was immersed in a sea of love. At that very moment, my heart was changed. Yes, it happened that quickly. One moment I was blind, hard-hearted, rebellious, stubborn and cold. The next moment, my eyes could see, my heart was soft and the warmth of God's love overwhelmed me. The people who had brought me to the church that night were absolutely astounded. I don't know what they expected when they invited me to come, but what happened to me surprised them utterly. I walked out of that church in Ottawa, and as we walked up the street to our car, I turned to them and, with tears running down my face, I said, "All I want to do is spend the rest of my life telling others about Jesus." Neither they nor I could understand how in one moment a heart that was so full of bitterness, anger, rebellion and sin could be so full of love, tenderness and joy.

That night, the God that I hated so much, turned my life upside down. He heard the cry of my heart and in an instant He transformed my life. Not only did God honour my initial commitment to Him, He heard my heart's desire to share the good news of Jesus with others. I didn't know when I said those words how much my life would change. Nine years later, I was ordained an Anglican Priest. I have spent the last twenty-five years as a layman and as a priest, telling others in the best way that I can, of the Father's tender love and mercy. There have been many joys in the years leading up to my ordination and after, but in those years I have also had a fair share of trial and tribulation. I expect it is some of these things that enable me to share with you about the Cross. I met Jesus at the cross—the cross that I hated. But it was the cross that transformed me and continues to transform me to this day. As with Dismas, mine was a cry from a lost soul to the heart of the Saviour, and as happened two thousand years ago, Jesus responded.

He continues to respond to the lost, if only they have the courage to cry out. He wants to restore people to His Father. He yearns to work that transformation in each of our lives. All it takes is your invitation to Him, an invitation to Him to come in to your heart. Your invitation could be like this:

> *"Lord Jesus Christ, Forgive me for all the sins I have committed. I repent of those actions. Forgive me for closing You out of my life for so long. I have heard You knocking at the door of my heart, and I invite You to come into my life as my Lord now. Make me the kind of person that You want me to be. Thank you for remembering me and I ask You to help me serve You all my life. Amen."*

If you have prayed this prayer, our Lord Jesus has heard the cry of your heart. Your transformation from a sinner to a child of God is instantaneous. Learning to walk as a child of God is a lifetime adventure. I encourage you to find a Bible, and a Church that preaches the Word of God. Learn to walk with God who loves you with a passion that will never grow cold. As you begin your personal journey, may God grant you the grace never to let go of His invisible hand.

Jesus brought Dismas back to God. He saved him from eternal death and blotted out his multitude of sins. Jesus did even more than that, though, He promised him Paradise. He promised that he would be in a place where there would be no more tears, or sorrows, or suffering, for God was making all things new. I don't think that promise was reserved only for Dismas. I think it's for every believer who ever cries out to God with childlike faith. The cry of the thief opened for him the door to the kingdom of God. I believe that God is listening to that same cry today. Charles Spurgeon, the great preacher of the last century, wrote these fine words:

> When Jesus arrived back in heaven after completing his work on earth, he brought with him the newly-converted Dismas. Why? I think the Saviour took him with him as a specimen of what he meant to do. He seemed to say to all the heavenly powers, "I bring a sinner with me; he is a sample of all the rest."[3]

In the introduction to this book, I told you that I had three audiences in mind. This book is for those who have always stumbled over the cross or found the message of the cross repulsive. I hope and pray that now you know it is an instrument of God's tender love. For those of you who wonder if we still need "the old rugged Cross," there is no other answer to humanity's problem with sin and death except "the old rugged Cross." For those of you who know, love and walk with Jesus, I hope and pray that this book has reaffirmed the commitment that you have made to the risen Christ. If it has, then I invite you to share the news of the risen Christ with others. Be salt and light in the world that God has called us to love and serve. Jesus' ministry was to bring comfort to those who mourn. He came to bestow a crown of beauty, instead of ashes, and a garment of praise, instead of a spirit of despair. As did Dismas, let us base our hope of salvation on God's eternal love, on God's mercy, God's tenderness, God's compassion, and most of all, on the sacrifice of His Son. As we finish our journey together, I thank you for travelling this road with me. My hope and prayer is that the grace of God has inspired you to a new awareness of His love and mercy. Remember that on the Cross of Reception, Dismas died *to* sin. On the Cross of Rejection, Gestas died *full of* sin. On the Cross of Redemption, Jesus died *for* sin.

The hymnwriter Richard Burnham expressed this truth in the powerful words of "Jesus, Thou Art The Sinner's Friend":

Jesus, Thou art the sinner's Friend,
As such I look to Thee
Now, in the fullness of thy love
O Lord, Remember Me.

Remember, Thy Pure Word of Grace,
Remember Calvary's Tree
Remember all Thy Dying Groans
And Then, Remember me.

Thou Wondrous Advocate with God,
I yield my Soul to Thee;
While Thou art pleading on the Throne,
Dear Lord, Remember me.

Lord, I am guilty; I am vile
But Thy Salvation's Free;
Then, in Thine all Abounding Grace
Dear Lord, Remember me.

Howe'er Forsaken or Despised
Howe'er Oppressed I be,
Howe'er Forgotten here on earth,
Do Thou, Remember me.

And when I close my eyes in Death
And Human help shall Flee
Then, Then, My Dear Redeeming God
Then, Remember Me.[4]

If it were possible to step into the shoes of Dismas or Gestas, two thousand years ago, which of the two crosses would you embrace? Would you be found on the *Cross of Rejection*, turning away from the only One who could truly save you? Or would you be found on the *Cross of Reception*, turning your heart to the One who is on the *Cross of Redemption*, the only One who could truly save you? Which Cross will you choose? Only you can make that decision; only you can make that choice!

NOTES

Writing on this subject is immense, but the following are works I have found helpful in this project. Humbly I express my deepest gratitude to the many Christian writers who have written so knowledgeably about the Cross. Your words, wisdom and insights were my guiding light as I sought to express in this work the truths I discovered at the foot of Calvary Hill. Please forgive this novice writer if I have unwittingly used any of your words of wisdom imprecisely.

INTRODUCTION

[1] Henri Nouwen, *Reflections on Theological Education,* cited by Philip Yancy in *Soul Survivor* (New York: Doubleday, 2001), 298.

[2] Philip Yancey, *Soul Survivor: how my faith survived the church* (New York: Doubleday, 2001), 262.

[3] Don Francisco, *Too Small a Price* (Coronation Music Ltd., 1978)

CHAPTER 2

[1] Lenore Majoros, *Celebrating the Centennial—A Souvenir of the First 100 Years,* (Kingston, Ont.: Parish Council, Church of the Good Thief, 1994), 11.

[2] Michael Card, *A Violent Grace* (Portland, Oreg.: Multnomah Publishers Inc., 2000), 106.

[3] Herschel Hobbs, *The Crucial Words from Calvary* (Grand Rapids, Mich.: Baker Book House, 1959), 29.

[4] Helmut Thielicke, *How the World Began* (Minneapolis, Minn.: Augsburg Fortress Press, 1961), 62.

[5] Christopher Idle, compiler, *Stories of Our Favourite Hymns* (Grand Rapids, Mich.: William B. Eerdmans, 1980), 10.

[6] William Temple, quoted in John Stott, *The Cross of Christ* (Downers Grove, Ill.: InterVarsity Press, 1986),197.

[7] Charles E. Wolfe, *The Seven Words from the Cross* (Lima, Ohio: C.S.S. Publishing Company, 1980), 33.

[8] Richard Hoefler, *At Noon on Friday* (Lima, Ohio: C.S.S. Publishing Company, 1990), 11.

[9] Hoefler, *At Noon on Friday,* 13.

CHAPTER 3

[1] J.D. Douglas and N. Hillyer, eds. *New Bible Dictionary, 2nd ed.* (Tyndale House Publishers, 1962), 373-374.

[2] Ibid., 374.

[3] Ibid., 374.

[4] <www.stsci.edu>

[5] <www.ibiblio.org>

[6] C.S. Lewis, *Mere Christianity* (London: William Collins Sons and Co Ltd., 1943; 1978), 52.

[7] Emil Brunner, *The Mediator,* tr. Olive Wyon, (Philadelphia, Pa.:Westminster Press, 1927; 1947), 435.

[8] John Stott, *The Cross of Christ* (Downers Grove, Ill.: InterVarsity Press, 1986), 1;11.

[9] J.I. Packer, "What Did the Cross Achieve?" *Tyndale Bulletin* 25 (1974), 3.

[10] P.T. Forsyth, *The Cruciality of the Cross* (London: Hodder & Stoughton, 1909), 44-45 and *The Work of Christ* (London: Hodder & Stoughton, 1910), 53.

[11] Stephen Neill, *"Jesus and History,"* in *Truth of God Incarnate,* ed. E.M.B. Green (London: Hodder & Stoughton, 1984), 80.

[12] William Barclay, *Crucified and Crowned* (London: SCM, 1961), 130.

[13] Michael Green, *The Empty Cross of Christ* (London: Hodder and Stoughton, 1984), 11.

[14] Martyn Lloyd-Jones, *The Cross: God's Way of Salvation* (Westchester, Ill.: Crossway Books, 1986), 18; 28-29.

[15] Stott, *The Cross of Christ*, 20.

[16] Richard John Neuhaus, *Death on a Friday Afternoon* (New York: Basic Books, 2000), 16-17.

[17] Henri Blocher, *Evil and the Cross,* tr. David G. Preston, (1994; Inter-Varsity Press, 1994), 49.

[18] Elie Wiesel, *Night*, tr. Stella Rodway (New York: Bantam Books, 1958; 1982), 62.

[19] Stott, *The Cross of Christ*, 336-337.

[20] Paul Tucker, *Jesus Crucified for Me* (London: Evangelical Press, 1966) 23.

[21] Stott, *The Cross of Christ*, 96.

[22] Douglas and Hillyer, *New Bible Dictionary,* 643-644.

[23] Ibid., 643.

[24] J.I. Packer, *Concise Theology* (Wheaton, Ill.: Tyndale House, 1993), 261.

[25] Packer, *Concise Theology,* 261-262

[26] The Book of Common Prayer, Article XXII (Toronto: Anglican Book Centre, 1962).

[27] J.I. Packer, *Concise Theology,* 262-263.

CHAPTER 4

[1] R. Bucklin, "The Legal and Medical Aspects of the Trial and Death of Christ, reprinted from Medicine," *Science and the Law*, January 1970, 10:14-26 (Sweet & Maxwell Ltd., 1970).

[2] M. Hengel, *Crucifixion in the Ancient World and the Folly of the Message of the Cross,* tr. John Bowden, (Minneapolis, Minn.: Augsburg Fortress Press, 1977).

[3] J. McDowell, *Evidence that Demands a Verdict: Historical Evidences for the Christian Faith* (Nashville: Thomas Nelson Inc., 1979)

[4] F. Josephus, *Jewish Wars*, tr. H. St. J. Thackeray (Cambridge, Mass.: Harvard University Press, 1989), 7:203.

[5] G. Friedrich, *Theological Dictionary of the New Testament*, (Grand Rapids: William B. Eerdmans, 1972).

[6] P. Barbet: *A Doctor at Calvary: The Passion of our Lord Jesus Christ as Described by a Surgeon* (New York: P.J. Kennedy & Sons, 1953).

[7] N.P. DePasquale and G.E. Burch, "Death by Crucifixion," *American Heart Journal* 66 (3), 1963.

[8] M. Lucado, *He Chose the Nails* (Nashville: Word Publishing, 2000), 45.

[9] Stott, *The Cross of Christ*, 68.

[10] <www.cnn.com> (May 10, 2002).

[11] R. Bucklin, "The Legal and Medical Aspects of the Trial and Death of Christ," reprinted from *Medicine, Science and the Law,* January 1970, 10:14-26 (Sweet & Maxwell Ltd., 1970).

[12] *New Bible Dictionary.*

[13] Peter Green, *Watchers by the Cross* (London: Longmans Green & Co., 1934), 27.

[14] Stott, *The Cross of Christ*, 98.

[15] Octavius Winslow, *No Condemnation in Christ Jesus* (Carlisle, Pa.: Banner of Truth, 1857; 1991).

[16] P.T. Forsyth, *The Work of Christ* (London: Hodder & Stoughton, 1938), 108.

[17] David L. McKenna, *Mark*. The Communicator's Commentary Series. (Waco, Texas: Word Books, 1982), 177.

[18] Donald English, *The Message of Mark*. The Bible Speaks Today Series. (Downers Grove, Ill.: InterVarsity Press, 1992), 159-160.

[19] Stott, *The Cross of Christ*, 37.

[20] John Wimber, *Equipping the Saints,* Volume 2, No. 2, Spring 1998, (Vineyard Ministries International, 1998), 55-56.

[21] Stott, *The Cross of Christ*, 65.

[22] W.D. Edwards, W.J. Gabel and F.E. Hosmer, "On the Physical Death of Jesus Christ," *Journal of the American Medical Association,* March 21 255 (11): 1455-63, 1986).

CHAPTER 5

[1] *Victoria Times Colonist.* Saturday, March 30th, 2002.

[2] <www.smart.net/`tak/patrons/thomas1.html>

[3] <www.catholic-form.com/saints/saintp07.htm>

[4] John Stott, *The Message of Acts—The Spirit, The Church and the World* The Bible Speaks Today Series. (Downers Grove, Ill.: InterVarsity Press, 1990), 168.

[5] <www.catholic-form.com/saints/saintp12.htm>

[6] The Book of Common Prayer (Toronto: Anglican Book Centre, 1962), 71.

CHAPTER 6

[1] Helen Franzee Bower, "No. 2751" in Paul Lee Tan, ed. *Encyclopedia of 7,007 Illustrations* (Rockville: Assurance Publishers, 1990).

[2] J.R. Miller, "No. 5307" in Paul Lee Tan, ed. *Encyclopedia of 7,007 Illustrations* (Rockville, Ga.: Assurance Publishers, 1990).

[3] Charles Spurgeon, *Sermon No. 2078* delivered on April 7th, 1889 at the Metropolitan Tabernacle, Newington, London. <www.spurgeon.org/sermons/ 2078.htm>

[4] Richard Burnham, "Jesus, Thou art the Sinner's Friend," quoted in *The Cross—An Anthology* (Nashville, Tenn.: Thomas Nelson, 2003), 113-114.

"Jesus, Remember Me"
Study Guide

This Study Guide was developed for individual use or for use in small group settings or in a Bible Study Group. If you are a member of a group, you are encouraged to discuss your answers with each other. It is hoped this guide will assist all users in theological reflection.

CHAPTER 1:
A HIDDEN TREASURE IN THE GOSPEL OF LUKE

1. What is the underlying theme in each of the four Gospel accounts and to whom were the Gospels written? (Pg. 27-28)

2. What are the characteristics that identify Luke's Gospel as the "universal Gospel?" (Pg. 27-28; 30-32; Lk 1:1-4; Lk 13:29; Isa 40:3-5; Lk 3:4-6)

3. What are some of the unique emphases in Luke's Gospel? (Pg. 28-29)

4. There are two parables and a story, which are told only in Luke's Gospel. What are they, and what do you think was Luke's purpose in including them? (Pg. 29-30)

5. In what ways do you think that the Gospel written by Luke differs from the accounts given by the other Gospel writers concerning the two men who were crucified with Jesus? (Pg. 30; Matt 27:44; Mk 15:32(b); John 19:18)

6. What is the golden thread running through the Gospel of Luke? What examples can you give to illustrate your answer? (Pg.30-32; Lk 1:31; Lk 2:10-11; Lk 4:18-19; Lk 4:21)

CHAPTER 2:
THE CROSS OF RECEPTION

1. Did Jesus know the two men who were crucified beside Him? What were the reasons that they were sentenced to die by crucifixion? What does tradition tell us about these two men?" (Pg. 33-34; Lk 23:39-43)

2. Jesus prayed this prayer from the Cross: 'Father, forgive them, for they don't know what they are doing.' Who do you think Jesus included in this prayer of forgiveness? Why do you think He was

so generous? (Pg. 36-37; Lk 23:34; Matt 27:18; Acts 3:17; Isa 50:6; Lk 5:24; Lk 23:24; Lk 6:27-28)

3. What reasons does the author offer to explain the change in Dismas' heart? Why does he refer to Dismas' profession of faith as "one of the most astonishing events recorded in all of Scripture?" What is your reaction to Jesus' promise to Dismas that he would be in Paradise with Him? (Pg.38-41; Lk 6: 27-28; Luke 23:40; Prov 9:10; 19:23; Lk 23:41; 2 Cor. 7:10;Lk 23:41b; Lk 23:42)

4. In the section on the "Joys of Reception" we learn about salvation. What do we have to admit, and what do we have to offer God to receive His gift of salvation? What do we learn about the nature of God in this section? (Pg. 41-47; Eph 2:8-9; Isa 64:6; Lk 10:27; Rom 5:6; Titus 3:3-7; Lk 15:7)

5. From the story of Dismas we learn about the "Gifts of Grace" that God gives to those who seek Him. What are these? Show how God bestowed each of these gifts on Dismas. (Pg. 47-53; Heb 11:1, 6; Isa 1:18; Ps 103:11-14; Isa 43:25; 1 John 1:8-9; 1John 2: 1-2; Rev 2:7; John 14:1-3)

6. What did Jesus mean in Matthew's Gospel when he said we need to become like little children? What can we be absolutely sure of when we turn to God and open our hearts to Him? (Pg. 53-56; Mt. 18:2-4; Ro 10:9-13; Ro 8:15-17; Eph 1:3-8; Mt 21:31; Mt 5:3, 6, 8)

CHAPTER 3:
THE CROSS OF REJECTION

1. What was Gestas' attitude to Jesus? What did Gestas seek from Jesus? (Pg. 58; Lk 23:39b)

2. How is "Fear of the Lord" used in Scripture? Why do those who believe in Jesus have no reason to fear? Which is the most

treasured of God's gifts to humanity? (Pg. 59-61; Jer 2:19; Gen 3:10; Prov 29:25; 1 John 4:15-18; John 3:16)

3. Many people reject Jesus' offer of salvation; what is the most common reason for this? What do you believe? (Pg. 61- 63; Acts 4:12; Rev 21:1-4)

4. What is the significance of the Great "I AM" statements found in John's Gospel and the book of Revelation? Why can we not say that Jesus was only a great moral teacher? What separates Christianity from the other religions of the world? (Pg. 63-65; John 14:6; 6:35; 8:58; 9:5; 10:7,11; 11:25; 15:5; Rev 1:8,17; Phil 2:6-11)

5. Another common reason given for rejecting Jesus is the cross itself. What did Jesus say about His death on the cross? What did the Apostles, and renowned scholars and historians of the Christian faith say about the Cross? What is the common dominant expression used by all eight of the scholars quoted here? (Pg. 66-70; John 10: 14-15, 17-18; 3:14, Mk 10:45, Acts 2:36; 4:10-11; Gal 2:20; Heb 7:27; Col 2:13-15; 1 Peter 2:24)

6. Rewrite the Apostle Paul's declaration about the Cross (1 Corinthians 1:18-31) in your own words. How did the Greek and Jewish people of Paul's day regard the cross? Why is preaching the true message of the cross today as difficult as it was in the first century? What was the focus of the Apostles' preaching? (Pg. 71-74; 1 Cor 1:18-31; 2:2; Gal 6:14))

7. The existence of suffering, evil, injustice and destruction in the world is often another reason for rejecting Jesus. People ask how God can allow such terrible things to happen in our world. How does the Christian answer such questions? (Pg. 75-84; Gen 2:15-17; 3:8-12; Job 19:25-29)

8. What does the Bible say about the consequences of rejecting the death of Jesus as the atonement for the sins of the world? If we

reject the salvation of the cross, what else are we rejecting? (Pg. 84-90; Rom 12:1-2; John 5:14/ 8:11; Gen 4:7; Rom 7:25; 1John 3:9; Lk 6:42; 23:41)

9. Why is it that many people today reject the idea that when we die, we will have to account to God for our lives? How would you respond to those who say God's character underwent a change between the Old and the New Testaments? Why is God's judgment just and how will that judgment be carried out? How can we be prepared for our judgment when it comes? (Pg. 90-99; Gen 18:16-33; Ex 34:6-7; Matt 16:27; Rom 2:6; 2 Cor 5:10; Rev 22:12; 1 Cor 4:5b; Matt 12:36-37;Rev 21: 6-8; 1 Cor 4:3-5; John 5:22)

CHAPTER 4:
THE CROSS OF REDEMPTION

1. What is the first significant event that took place during the Passover meal Jesus shared with his disciples in the Upper Room? How did this event clearly indicate the significance Jesus attached to His death? What were the differences and the similarities between the covenant God entered into with the Israelites and the new covenant God established by this event? (Pg. 105-108; Lk 22:8-20; 1 Cor 11:25-26; Ex 24:8; Jer 31:31-40)

2. Why did Jesus select Judas as one of His twelve chosen apostles? Why did Judas betray Jesus? What do we learn from Judas' actions? (Pg. 108-112; John 13:22-31; Matt 26:14-16, 24; John 17:12; John 13:5; Ps 41:9; Matt 27:9-10)

3, Why were the Sanhedrin and the Pharisees so determined that Jesus had to die? Why is the trial they carried out described as "a mockery?" In what ways was Jesus so unlike the Messiah they wanted? Describe the four attempts made by Pilate to release Jesus (Pg. 112-120; John 18:19-21; Ex 23:15; Deut 17:6-7; Mark 14:61b-62; Ex 3:13-14; Mark 14:62, 65; Lk 23:1-2)

4. What is God's solution to our "lostness"? What does Paul's famous description of God's love for each of us in Romans 8: 31b-39 reveal to you? (Pg. 120-124; 1 Peter 1:18-20; Eph 1:4-8; Rev 13:8; Rom 8:31b-39)

5. Why did Jesus come into this world? Where did the changing point of Jesus' ministry take place? What theme now becomes evident in Jesus' ministry? What did Jesus accomplish for us that we could not accomplish for ourselves? Why is Jesus referred to as "the Lamb of God?" What is the difference between the sacrifices offered by the Levitical priesthood of the Old Testament and the sacrificial death of Jesus? (Pg. 124-130; Lk 2:34-35; John 1:29; Mk 8:29-32, 38; 10:33-34, 45; Eph 1:7; Ro 3:24, 8:23; Col 1:13-14; Gal 3:13; 1 Pet 1:18-29, 2:24-25; Heb 4:14, 8:10; Rev 5:9-12)

6. What does it mean to "be reconciled with God?" Why is "sin" such an unpopular topic today? What sin caused the original separation between God and humanity? What does "atonement" mean? What was the Old Testament rite of Atonement? Why was it limited? On page 136 sin is defined as "the human will colliding with the divine will" and as "a state of being alienated from God, from others and even from ourselves." Why do we try to escape from admitting that we are sinners? What are the five different meanings for sin we find when we read the Epistles? (Pg 130-139; Col 1:21-22; Heb 9:2-4, 11-14; 4:14-16; Col 1:18-20; 2 Cor 5: 18-19, 21; Judges 2:10-15; Gen 3; Heb 10:14; John 1:29)

7. How does the New Testament differ from the Old Testament with regard to "forgiveness?" What does the Lord's Prayer say? How are our lives limited by an unforgiving heart? by not forgiving ourselves? What is the higher standard Jesus calls us to? What do the apostles Peter and Paul teach us about forgiveness? (Pg.139-141; Lk 11:4; Matt 18:21; Lk 23:34; 2 Cor 5:21)

8. Look at the explanation of "justification" on page 142, lines 4-8, and then describe in your own words what the apostle Paul meant in Romans 5:19. What is it that we must acknowledge in order to realize this gift of righteousness? How has this helped you understand the promise Jesus made to the dying Dismas? (Pg. 142-143; Rom 8:1; 5:1,19; Isa 53:3-6; Rom 5:8-10)

9. After eating the Passover meal, Jesus and His disciples go to the Garden of Gethsemane. Jesus separates Himself from His disciples and prays. He asks, "Father, if you are willing, take this cup from me; yet not my will, but yours be done." What is this cup, and what did it mean for Jesus? How would you compare the events in the Garden of Eden with Jesus' Garden of Gethsemane experience? What are some of the Scriptures in the New Testament Epistles that affirm that death was defeated by the death of Jesus? (Pg. 144-151; 1 Pet 3:18; Rom 6:10, 14:9; 1 Cor 15:54-57, 26; Rev 20:14;Matt 26:38, 40-41, 42; Lk 22:44; Isa 51:17; Ezek 23:32-33; Gal 3:13; 2 Cor 5:21; Ps 22:1; Matt 27:46; 2 Cor 5:19)

CHAPTER 5:
EVIDENCE OF THE RESURRECTION

1. Why did the writers of the New Testament not need to prove Jesus' resurrection beyond any reasonable doubt? Why do the writers from Genesis to Revelation never attempt to prove the existence of God? Do all the witnesses to an event (for example, a traffic accident) tell identical stories? What is the one thing on which all witnesses agree? What are the similarities and what are the differences in the four Gospel accounts of the empty tomb on that Easter Sunday morning? In the Emmaus Road appearance by Jesus when was it that the two disciples recognized the risen Jesus? What was the similarity between the Emmaus Road appearance and Jesus' appearance to the disciples reassembled in the Upper

Room? What happened to Peter to make us believe that it was specially included for Peter's sake? (Pg. 153-162; Deut 17:6; Matt 28:1-10, 18-20; Mk 16:1-8; Lk 24: 5b-7; Lk 24: 13-35; John 20:1-31, 21:1-23)

2. What was it that the early disciples were never accused of in the history of the early Church? What were the means the Jewish authorities used in their attempts to eliminate Jesus as the Messiah? What words did Paul use to describe how he was converted and called to be an apostle? How do the sufferings and deaths of Peter, Thomas and Paul attest to their belief in the risen Jesus and to their changed lives? How does the prophet Jeremiah record that God honours seekers by revealing Himself to them? How does the Nicene Creed affirm the Resurrection? (Pg. 162-168; Matt 27:62-65; Matt 28:2-4, 12-15; 2 Cor 11:22-29; Jer 29:13-14; 1 Cor 15:19)

3. What is your response to the words: "Christ has died, Christ is risen, and Christ will come again?" (Pg. 165-169)

CHAPTER 6:
WHICH CROSS WILL YOU CHOOSE?

1. What would your reaction be if you were confronted with the three crosses on Calvary Hill? Does Jesus force us to accept Him? What is the significant Scripture from Revelation that supports the message that Jesus refused to force anyone to accept Him? How can we be so sure that if we have extended the invitation to Jesus to come into our lives, we will not be alone when we die? What are some of the things that will happen to us after Jesus comes into our lives? Which Old Testament prophet assures us that when we have embraced the things of God, we will become all that God intended us to be? Why should we not take the risk of presuming on the grace of God? What is the single step we need to take for Jesus to transform our lives? If we hear the

voice of God, why should we not harden our hearts towards Him? (Pg.170-175; Heb 12:25; Rev 3:20; Ps 23:4, 6b; Jer 29:11-14; Mk 8: 34-37; 2 Cor 4:4; Heb 3:12-15)

2. When did you become fully aware that Christ died for you?

3. How does the death of Christ affect your life?

4. What do the words, "Jesus, Remember Me" mean to you?

SELECT BIBLIOGRAPHY

Writing on this subject is immense, but the following are works I have found helpful in this project.

Barbet, P., *A Doctor at Calvary: The Passion of Our Lord Jesus Christ as Described by a Surgeon* (P. J. Kennedy & Sons, 1953).

Barclay, William, *The Gospel of Matthew. Daily Study Bible, Revised Edition* (The Westminster Press, 1975).

— *The Gospel of Mark. Daily Study Bible, Revised Edition* (The Westminster Press, 1975).

— *The Gospel of Luke. Daily Study Bible, Revised Edition* (The Westminster Press, 1975).

— *The Gospel of John. Daily Study Bible, Revised Edition* (The Westminster Press, 1975).

Blocher, Henri, *Evil and the Cross,* tr. David G. Preston (1994; InterVarsity Press, 1994).

Boice, James Montgomery and Ryken, Philip Graham, *Jesus on Trial* (Crossway Books, 2002).

Bonhoeffer, Dietrich, *Meditations on the Cross,* tr. Douglas W. Stott (1996; Westminster John Knox Press, 1998).

— *The Cost of Discipleship,* tr. R.H. Fuller (1937; Macmillan, 1959).

Bucklin, R., "The Legal and Medical Aspects of the Trial and Death of Christ," reprinted from *Medicine, Science and the Law,* January 1970, 10:14-26 (Sweet & Maxwell Ltd., 1970).

Card, Michael, *A Violent Grace* (Multnomah Publishers Inc., 2000).

Carey, George, *The Gate of Glory* (1986; Wm. B. Eerdmans Publishing Co. 1994).

Clow, W. M., *The Day of the Cross,* reprint of 1909 ed. (Baker Book House, 1954).

Colson, Charles and Pearcey, Nancy, *The Problem of Evil* (Tyndale House Publishers, 2001).).

Crosby, Michael H., *The Seven Last Words* (Orbis Books, 1994).

DePasquale, N.P. and Burch, G.E., *Death by Crucifixion* (American Heart Journal 66(3), 1963).

Douglas, J. D. (Organizing Editor) and Hillyer, N. (Revision Editor), *New Bible Dictionary,* Second Edition, (Tyndale House Publishers, 1982).

Edwards, W. D., Gabel, W.J. and Hosmer, F.E.: "On The Physical Death of Jesus Christ" (*Journal of the American Medical Association* March 21 255(11):1455-63, 1986).

Ford, Herschel W., *Seven Simple Sermons on the Saviour's Last Words* (Zondervan Publishing House, 1953).

Friedrich, G. (editor), Kittel, G. (editor), Bromiley, G.W. (transl), *Theological Dictionary of the New Testament* (Wm. B. Eerdmans Publishing Company, 1972).

Girard, Rene, *I See Satan Fall Like Lightning* (Orbis Books, 2001).

Goodier, Alban (Archbishop), *The Passion and Death of our Lord Jesus Christ* (P. J. Kennedy & Sons, 1959).

Gordon, Bob, *The Cross (The Explaining Series)* (Sovereign World Ltd., 1991).

Gorman, Ralph, *The Last Hours of Jesus* (Sheed and Ward, 1960).

Green, Michael, Th*e Empty Cross of Jesus* (Hodder & Stoughton, 1984).

— *You Must Be Joking* (Hodder & Stoughton, 1976).

Green, Peter, *Watchers by the Cross: thoughts on the seven last words* (Longmans Green, 1934).

Hendricksen, William, *The Gospel of Matthew* (Baker Book House, 1973).

— *The Gospel of Mark* (Baker Book House, 1975).

— *The Gospel of Luke* (Baker Book House, 1978).

— *The Gospel of John* (Baker Book House, 1953)

Hengel, Martin, *Crucifixion in the Ancient World and the Folly of the Message of the Cross,* tr. Bowden, John. (Augsburg Fortress Press, 1977).

Hodges, H.A., *The Pattern of Atonement* (SCM Press Ltd., 1955).

Hoefler, Richard, *At Noon on Friday* (CSS Publishing Company, 1990).

Idle, Christopher, compiler, *Stories of Our Favourite Hymns* (William B. Eerdmans Publishing Company, 1980).

Josephus, F., *Jewish War,* tr. H. St. J. Thackeray. (Harvard University Press, 1989).

Lucado, Max, *And the Angles Were Silent* (Multnomah Press, 1992).

— *Six Hours One Friday* (Word Publishing, 1989).

— *No Wonder They Call Him Savior* (Kingsway Communications, 1986).

— *He Chose The Nails* (Word Publishing, 2000).

Larson, Bruce, *The Communicator's Commentary Series—Luke,* (Word Books, 1984).

Lloyd-Jones, D. Martyn, *The Cross* (Crossway Books, 1987).

— *Studies in the Sermon on the Mount* (Wm. B. Eerdmans Publishing Company, 1984).

Loane, Marcus L., *The Hill of the Cross* (Oliphants, 1968).

MacArthur, John, *The Murder of Jesus* (W Publishing Group, 2002).

McGrath, Alister, *The Enigma of the Cross* (Hodder & Stoughton, 1987).

Majoros, Lenore, *Celebrating the Centennial: A Souvenir of the First 100 Years,* 1994.

McDowell, J., *Evidence that Demands a Verdict: Historical Evidences for the Christian Faith* (Thomas Nelson Inc., 1979).

Mills, James R., *Memoirs of Pontius Pilate* (Ballantine Books, 2001).

Morris, Leon, *The Apostolic Preaching of the Cross* (1955; Wm. B. Eerdmans Publishing Co., 1976).

— *The Cross of Jesus,* (Wm. B. Eerdmans Publishing Co., 1988).

Neuhaus, Richard John, *Death on a Friday Afternoon* (Basic Books, 2000).

Packer, James, *Concise Theology* (Tyndale House, 1993).

Pink, Arthur, *The Seven Sayings of the Saviour on the Cross* (Baker Book House, 1958).

Rees, Edward J., *Christ Speaks from Calvary* (Cokesbury Press, 1935).

Stott, John, *The Cross of Christ* (InterVarsity Press, 1986).

Swindol, Charles, *The Darkness and the Dawn* (W Publishing Group, 2001).

Tan, Paul Lee, *Encyclopedia of 7,700 Illustrations,* 11th Printing, (Assurance Publishers, 1990).

The Book of Common Prayer, 1962, Canada. (Anglican Book Centre).

Tucker, Paul, *Jesus Crucified for Me* (Evangelical Press, 1966).

Turnbull, Ralph, *The Seven Words from the Cross* (Baker Book House, 1956).

Wimber, John, *Equipping the Saints* Volume 2, No. 2, Spring 1998, (Vineyard Ministries International, 1998).

Wolfe, Charles, *The Seven Words from the Cross* (C.S.S. Publishing Company, 1980).

Wright, Tom, *The Crown and the Fire* (SPCK, 1992)

Yancy, Philip, *What's So Amazing About Grace* (Zondervan, 1997)

— *Soul Survivor,* (Doubleday, 2001).